Data Decoded

A GenZ Guide to Business Analytics

Includes topics on INTELLIGENT AGENTS and ETHICAL ASPECTS

Dr Meera Suresh
Dr Lakshmi Shankar Iyer

INDIA · SINGAPORE · MALAYSIA

This book has been published with all efforts taken to make the material error-free after the consent of the author. However, the author and the publisher do not assume and hereby disclaim any liability to any party for any loss, damage, or disruption caused by errors or omissions, whether such errors or omissions result from negligence, accident, or any other cause.

While every effort has been made to avoid any mistake or omission, this publication is being sold on the condition and understanding that neither the author nor the publishers or printers would be liable in any manner to any person by reason of any mistake or omission in this publication or for any action taken or omitted to be taken or advice rendered or accepted on the basis of this work. For any defect in printing or binding the publishers will be liable only to replace the defective copy by another copy of this work then available.

Contents

Preface

With the huge volume of data generation with the proliferation of devices in all forms, there is a dire need to process data to make meaningful insights. In businesses, these insights would lead to effective decision making. Irrespective of the functions like Finance, Human Resources, Manufacturing, and Marketing, coupled with domains like Banking, Insurance, Airline, Telecom, Retail, Healthcare, Sports, Education and much more: there is a significant impact of analytics. This has led to the tech industry investing on smarter devices, processors to enable quick transactions and processes and efficient networks for data transmission.

In this tech era, every graduate student is required to understand the basics of analytics, their applications and associated trending areas. The origin of data, organisation of data and way to efficiently retrieve them to make quick decisions and reports are important to understand as well. As the graduates enter into the job market, these knowledge and skills would make a big difference in their employability quotient.

The objective of the book **'Data Decoded: A GenZ guide to Business Analytics'** is to help GenZ from varied backgrounds decode the 'World of Analytics' in a simple manner. The approach is to hand hold the readers towards the objective. The book would be a perfect fit for institutes, colleges and universities who would like to introduce 'Basics of Business Analytics' or 'Analytics for Business' courses during the first or second year.

In order to promote independent learning and help the instructors assess the students, assessment questions and caselets are included in the book.

ORGANIZATION OF THE BOOK

- **Logical Format.** The book follows a logical flow from the basics to the advanced topics. There are enough sub-sections, which breaks down the topics to make the learning in a modular fashion.
- **Numbering of Headings.** The numbering systems helps the learner quickly reach a sub-section for better exploration and access.
- **Key Content.** The book 'Data Decoded: A GenZ Guide to Business Analytics' is organized into five chapters.

  ✓ **Chapter 1, Introduction to Business Analytics** covers the basic concepts of analytics, types, applications, data sources, data quality, and the role of a business analytics in business and society. There are elaborate discussions with the support of case scenarios to emphasize the concept.

  ✓ **Chapter 2, Analytics Methodology** focuses on data collection, working on objectives of data analysis, methodology of analysis, data processing or cleaning, interpretation of data and concluding with a business solution. Multiple hands-on methodologies are identified to bring experiential learning to the learners.

  ✓ **Chapter 3, Visualization of Data** investigates the need for visualization, types of charts, right use of charts, and most importantly data summarization aspects. This chapter explores the scientific aspects of data visualization so that it would be help in interpretation of visual representations.

  ✓ **Chapter 4, Databases, Data warehousing and Data mining** covers the various types of data, sources of data, relational databases, data warehouses, types of databases and some data mining techniques. A detailed discussion on the characteristics of databases and architecture of data warehouse is presented in this chapter.

  ✓ **Chapter 5, Future Trends in Analytics** explores the application side of analytics through text mining, web analytics, social media analytics. A significant part of this chapter is focused upon intelligent agents and their types. The role of Artificial Intelligence in Business along with the ethical aspects is covered in detail as well.

ADDITIONAL RESOURCES

Learning gets completed with the right assessment and evaluation methods after the concepts are discussed by an instructor or through self-learning. The book caters to both the categories of learners. The following assessment tools appear in every chapter of **'Data Decoded: A GenZ guide to Business Analytics'.**

- ❖ **Multiple Choice Questions** help the learners to evaluate themselves on the critical thinking aspects and provides clarity on the concepts discussed in the chapter.
- ❖ **Content questions** in each chapter provides a summary which would cement the conceptual understanding of the learners. Each learner must be comfortable answering all the questions before moving on to the next chapter.
- ❖ **Points to be remembered** help the learners run through the significant topics and highlights the focus areas.

Acknowledgements

The book on **'Data Decoded: A GenZ guide to Business Analytics'** was ideated during a discussion on the need for a simple, comprehensive book on 'Analytics for Business', for learners who are eager to explore this world. While delivering the topics, it was observed that although the concepts remain the same, however, the discussion scenarios kept changing as per the changing business conditions. Class engagement was wonderful while the applications were brought forth from the news headlines. However, we understand that there is a need for a book which covers the basic concepts and keeps the students grounded to further build on the same.

First and foremost, we would like to thank the GOD Almighty for His guidance and strength throughout the writing of this book.

I, Meera Suresh acknowledge the constant support and encouragement from my parents, in-laws, my husband Suresh Prakash and son Karan Prakash. I thank my family for their patience and understanding during the long hours spent by me immersed in academic pursuit.

I, Lakshmi Shankar Iyer would like to express my deepest gratitude to my husband Shankar Iyer, sons Hari Shankar Iyer and Shiva Shankar Iyer for their unwavering support throughout this journey with a smile and boundless motivation. Also, I acknowledge the critique received from them at every stage during the course which helped shape up the book.

CHAPTER 01

Introduction to Business Analytics

Tagline – "Welcome to the world of Analytics"

PROLOGUE

The buzzword **Analytics** has caught the entire business world by storm. With the proliferation of data through multiple devices, businesses have found meaning by deriving insights for decision making by deploying the analytics concepts. Though there are tools immense which have flooded the market, it would be sensible to understand what is analytics all about and its applications across domains and functions.

CHAPTER OUTLINE

A. CONCEPTS OF ANALYTICS
B. BUSINESS ANALYTICS
C. TYPES OF ANALYTICS
D. APPLICATION FIELDS
E. ANALYTICS IN FUNCTIONAL AREAS
F. DATA SOURCES
G. DATA QUALITY
H. DEALING WITH MISSING OR INCOMPLETE DATA
I. ROLE OF DATA SCIENTIST IN BUSINESS AND SOCIETY

LEARNING OBJECTIVES

The objectives of this chapter are

- To introduce the learners to the world of analytics for business decision making.

- To elaborate on the various types of analytics, their applications across functions and domains.
- To discuss the data sources and data quality for effective and impactful decision making.

A. CONCEPTS OF ANALYTICS

"Information is the oil of the 21st century, and Analytics is the combustion engine." Peter Sondergaard, Senior Vice President and Global Head of Research at Gartner, Inc. Organisations across the business world generate huge volumes of data due to the proliferation of devices which are the sources of data. It is not optional for businesses any more to derive insights from the data for decision making. Businesses are mandated to unleash the power of data while effectively managing large volumes of data generated within the organisation. Businesses, Government and Society fall under the category of data generators. Analytics has enabled the process of leveraging the data to transform the same to business insights for private and public sector organisations. It is difficult for most organisations to catalogue and categorise the data as per their needs and frame the rules and processes for using the same for effective decision making. It is even challenging to translate that data into useful insights. But with the advent of data analytics, both the private and public sector organisations are capable of leveraging the transformation of data to meaningful insights.

1.1 ANALYTICS IN SEPHORA

Sephora is a cosmetics retailer and has many online and offline customers. By deploying analytics, they found that the customers use their smartphones to search for product reviews, recommendations, better prices while purchasing products in store. Based on this insight, the company developed a mobile app that provided product recommendations, reviews, and pricing information which helped customers make decisions while purchasing products. The app used facial recognition technology which customers used to virtually try on makeup products like lipsticks. The customers can see virtually how they appear by applying various lipstick shades and buy whatever looks best on them prior to the purchase process.

Using analytics, they understood the habits and behaviour patterns of in-store shoppers. Customer needs and preferences were fulfilled by using the data generated through the mobile app. Sephora was able to track the purchase and usage behaviour of customers offline. The mobile app tracked the online behaviour pattern. Based on the offline and online data the company was able to take decisions to achieve increased customer satisfaction. The company was able to provide relevant recommendations and offers based on product reviews by individual customers. Thus, the analytics applications in consumer behaviour helped Sephora achieve increased sales based on the data generated within the business itself.

B. BUSINESS ANALYTICS

Let us understand how traditional analytics is different from data analytics. These two terminologies are used interchangeably but there is a distinction between the two. Traditional analytics involves analysing large amounts of data gathered to derive insights and make predictions. Business analytics takes inputs from this but deploys the same in the context of business insights. Data mining, simulation, forecasting, data management and visualisation are some techniques to obtain meaningful insights from the data. Business analytics makes use of quantitative techniques, statistics, and operations research to create insights from data.

In other words, we can say Business analytics refers to gathering and processing of historical business data, analysing the data to understand the patterns and trends and making data driven decision based on the derived insights through analysis.

E-commerce giant Flipkart uses data analytics to gather better insights for various business activities. The company uses data analytics to help its sellers to arrive at a good understanding of the business during Big Billion Days which is typically run in festival seasons. Their focus is on popular categories like electronic products, apparels, and lifestyle products. Customer demand is predicted using the data collected from the order records and previous purchase behaviour. The insights help the seller maintain stock of products and manage inventory leading to improved customer satisfaction due to timely product delivery.

Most organisations generate large volumes of data as the processes have been automated due to improved technology infrastructure in the recent years. Some of the data include customer data or product data or transaction details for a period of time among others. This data would be put into good use only if analysis is conducted diligently. This will help organisations find a pattern in the purchase behaviour of consumers related to quantity, type and frequency of purchase. Comparative analysis across multiple months can be carried out in order to identify a pattern or trends. Analytics helps organisations understand customers, products and the overall business in a better way.

C. TYPES OF ANALYTICS

Having understood the Basics of Business Analytics, we shall understand the various types of Analytics. Broadly, Analytics can be classified into four types, namely - Descriptive, Diagnostic, Predictive and Prescriptive.

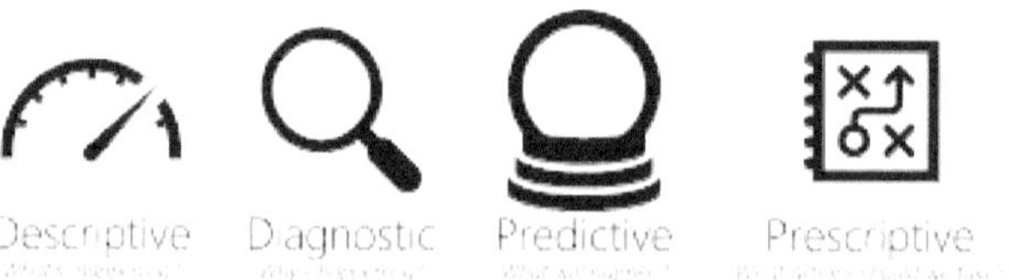

Figure 1: Types of Analytics

The four types can be briefly defined as:

      Descriptive Analytics : What happened?
      Diagnostic Analytics : Why did it happen?
      Predictive Analytics : What will happen?
      Prescriptive Analytics : What is to be done next?

C.1. Descriptive analytics is the most widely used analytics. It gathers data from various sources and generates meaningful insights from past actions. It helps in interpretation of historical data to have a better understanding of the changes that have occurred in a business. Descriptive analytics focuses on understanding and summarising patterns in the historical and present data. It does not attempt to analyse why something happened or will happen in future.

Organisations do not just consider the understanding from descriptive analytics but combine them with other types of analytics. It is used to produce reports, KPIs and business metrics which enables organisations to track performance and other trends. Data mining and data aggregation are the fundamental methods used in descriptive analytics. Netflix makes use of descriptive analytics to check which shows or movie genre interests the customers. The insights obtained will help in decision making for advertising, promotional campaigns, and the production houses to work with.

Descriptive analytics tends to answer the question "What has gone by?". It observes the past trends and summarises the historical data and identified patterns. These patterns help the analyst derive insights with regard to what has gone by in the business. Descriptive analytics aggregates data into crisper and meaningful information. This summary information helps the decision makers have a quick glance at the past performance as browsing through large volumes of data consumes time and effort. We often hire cabs for local commutation. Some of the players which fall under aggregators include Uber, Ola, Rapido among others. This mode has become one of the convenient and safe forms of transportation especially for women due to its inbuilt safety features.

Mola, a cab aggregator, wanted to make a mark in this industry. The company conducted its business using a mobile app. That is, the commuters had to download an app on their smartphones and through that the booking of cab, cancellation, inclusion of pickup and drop was possible. As the Google Maps was incorporated into the app, it was easier for the commuters to visibly see the movement of the cabs towards the pickup point. Customer data, their ride pattern, rating given all were tracked by Mola as the data was automatically captured in the servers. This data included the number of rides a cab took on a single day along with the time, location, customer details and the price involved.

Can this data be used by Mola for drawing insights? Let us consider the following questions to observe the ride behaviour:

a. Which time of the day the cabs are in high demand?
b. What is the average waiting duration by a commuter before the cab arrives to pick up?
c. Which are the popular destination commuters preferring to go during weekends?
d. What is the price variation at various time durations across locations?

Responses to these questions would summarise the gathered data. Patterns are derived after analysis in order to arrive at various insights. This is nothing but Descriptive analytics. The collected data can be represented visually using tools such as Microsoft Power BI, Qlik, IBM Cognos and Tableau. As pictures speak better than words, the visual representation has more impact on the reader's ability to understand and interpret the data to derive insights.

C.2. Diagnostic Analytics is a type of analytics which is used to find out why an activity occurred in the past. Companies can get insights into the reasons for patterns seen in their data by applying diagnostic analytics. It gives detailed insights into a particular problem. In addition, it examines external factors that may be influencing the patterns in data, looking for new sources to aid in drawing a larger picture, and then comparing the conclusions drawn with the original dataset. Data drilling and data mining are two strategies that can be used in diagnostic analytics.

Diagnostic analytics is usually performed using techniques like data discovery, drill-down, data mining, and correlations. It digs into data to understand the main causes of the events. It is useful in finding out what actions and events lead to a specific outcome. It uses a variety of methods like regression analysis, probabilities, likelihoods, filtering, time series analysis. Spotify uses diagnostic analytics when there is an event, like an album release, an extensive marketing campaign, or a tour, where you are trying to understand the impact on the output or your streams.

Diagnostic Analytics tends to answer the question "Why is a pattern observed?". It is that type of analytics which is built on top of descriptive analytics. It examines the data and understands the reason why an event occurred in the past. This can also be known as root cause analysis as it takes a deeper understanding of occurrence of an event or observation of a specific pattern.

Let us take the discussion on Mola forward to understand diagnostic analytics in a better way. The COO of Mola made a plan to reach a target of 60,000 rides per month across all cabs. The historical ride data captured through the app can be used to summarise the ride activity throughout the month. The COO makes an observation during the middle of the month that Mola has completed only 20,000 rides till date whereas the target is to reach 60,000 rides. The results are attained through Descriptive Analytics. Is it a cause for worry now as Mola seems to be underperforming? Based on the diagnostic analytics information, Mola has to find avenues to increase the number of rides in order to achieve the target amidst competition. Once the results of the analysis proves that Mola is underperforming, the COO would like to find out the root cause for the same.

A typical question would be "Why is Mola underperforming?". Strategies for improvement from this status need to be worked out from this insight. Let us assume that the COO finds out that most of the rides are ordered from the Eastern region of the city as compared to other regions. Diagnostic analytics would help the COO find out the reason for this pattern through market research. More dimensions like type of cab ordered, frequency of rides can be added too in order to conduct in-depth diagnosis.

There are limitations while we work through Descriptive and Diagnostic analytics as both the techniques involve uncovering hidden patterns only. They cannot provide actionable insights. This is achievable by Predictive and Prescriptive analytics.

C. 3. Predictive analytics deals with making predictions about future outcomes using historical data. Predictive analytics is an advanced form of analytics, it uses past and current data to forecast, understand behaviour and trends. It applies statistical modelling, data mining techniques and machine learning. Companies use predictive analytics to find patterns in the data to identify the likelihood of a particular event, understand the risks and opportunities. Consider a hotel which wants to estimate how many people will stay in the hotel in a festival season so that they can plan about the resources they need to meet demand. Motorists depend on GPS-enabled navigation apps to get from one place to another. Small businesses providing delivery services use GPS. Predictive analytics use the existing GPS-sourced travel data and map a potentially faster route. Marriott hotel is using predictive analytics to predict demand and customer behaviour. They considered the data containing details about how many times a person travels, is it for leisure or business and so on. By applying analytics, they predicted where there was demand for additional hotels too.

Predictive analytics tends to answer the question "What could probably happen in the future?". Due to its probabilistic nature, predictive analytics uses statistical techniques to build models based on historical data. These models help businesses predict future trends and forecast performance. As we observed earlier, Mola has gathered historical data about the number of rides done by the cabs, commuter behaviour and type of cabs or vehicles ordered. This data becomes valuable as the number of expected rides Mola has to anticipate on a particular day will help them strategize the pricing. If the COO is able to predict the surge in demand during a particular day or hour from a specific location, he/she could deploy additional cabs to this location at a specific time to meet commuter demand.

C. 4. Prescriptive Analytics helps to make better decisions about what the next set of actions should be. It can be any aspect of business such as preventing fraud, increasing efficiency, or increasing revenue. Prescriptive analytics conducts analysis of raw data and helps organisations make better decisions. It can be for any time horizon ranging from immediate to long term. Energy sectors use pipeline companies, gas producers, utility companies use prescriptive analytics to find factors that affect the price of oil and gas. Thus, energy sector has tapped the potential of prescriptive analytics.

Prescriptive analytics tends to answer the question "What is to be done next?". This provides suggestions or recommendations with a purpose to optimise business scenarios in a simulated environment. Interestingly, this technique also falls back on the historical data that includes prediction of what could probably happen in the future and suggesting the best way possible to achieve a goal as defined by the business. Once the COO observes a surge in demand from a particular location during a time period, it becomes important for the business to fulfil the demand within a stipulated time. Prescriptive analytics solutions take care of the best possible route amidst multiple options given the constraints in the road environment which includes traffic and other contingencies.

As one might have observed already, analytics is a process and progression from descriptive, diagnostic, predictive and prescriptive solutions for a business to take effective data driven decisions.

Exercise: Identify the applications of four types of analytics in the insurance domain. Prepare a write up of about 300 words justifying the same with a relevant business case.

D. APPLICATION FIELDS

Analytics is considered to be a horizontal application which cuts across various business domains. It has the capability of cutting across multiple functional areas of a business too. Every business domain and functional area generates data due to the aspect of technology enablement. Data generation takes place through business processes that have become an integral part of the system. Organisations spend money in IT infrastructure in order to ensure that the data generated gets stored in a secure manner.

The data thus stored can be used for deriving business insights if put into good use. It becomes the responsibility of a manager to identify use cases in a domain where the data could be used to make effective decisions for businesses. Application areas vary from transportation, healthcare, insurance, banking, airline, telecom, retail, education and much more. Some of the application fields are elaborated here.

a. Transportation: Companies in the travel sector can use analytics and design personalised travel packages with data collected about the travellers. It can improve transport problems like traffic congestion by better route planning, suggesting alternative routes and reducing the number of accidents and road mishaps.

b. Manufacturing: Data analytics helps the manufacturing industries get insights into which components fail most frequently. This information helps the industry take rectification steps early. It can combine existing data with predictive analytics to build an accurate projection of what purchasing trends will be. It is not just based on past sales, but also on processes leading to better risk management and less production waste, and better warehouse management.

c. Education: Data analytics is used in adaptive learning, new innovative methods to deliver classes. It helps in getting a detailed understanding of students and faculties. This in turn will improve the operational effectiveness of the institution. Various industry relevant courses are marketed, curricula are structured using analytics.

d. Health Care: Data analytics in healthcare can be used to discover treatment choices or answers for various illnesses. Health care organisations and practitioners can get detailed models for lowering costs and patient risk. In addition to the patient-centric benefits, analytics can reduce appointment no-shows, manage supply chain costs, prevent equipment breakdowns and decrease fraud.

e. Insurance: Analytics in the insurance sector can be used to improve risk assessment, enhance customer experience, and reduce most in claim processing. The underwriters can make predictions about customers' risk profile with greater accuracy. Use of analytics can minimise fraudulent claims, can save an insurer a significant amount in pay-outs. They enable the company to extend the benefit of competitive insurance premiums to all customers.

1.2 ANALYTICS AT APOLLO

Analytics can bring a dramatic improvement in the way hospitals operate. It can leverage the usage of IT to manage operations and deliver healthcare in a seamless manner and overcome the challenges faced. Since about the past 15 years, most of the healthcare centres and hospitals in India have had basic technology infrastructure. They had amenities like hardware, software, network setup and hospital staff were trained to use various technologies in the various operations. Most of the manual processes became automated and hospitals were sitting on a pile of data. Some of the services for which IT was deployed include online doctor appointments, maintaining patients records and billing processes.

Many hospitals have started applying analytics to get insights for better management of their resources. Apollo hospitals use analytics for both clinical and non-clinical activities. Use of analytics in Apollo resulted in making it a data-driven organisation. They have pioneered the concept of personalised health check-ups in India: instead of patients going for a general check-up proactively, personalised check-ups are recommended to individual patients using data analytics. Specific medicines are recommended for a particular disease that matches with patients who have similar health conditions. This has helped Apollo Hospitals to give patients quicker treatment with improved outcomes.

E. ANALYTICS IN FUNCTIONAL AREAS

E.1. Marketing Analytics

Marketing analytics is a type of analytics that makes use of data to understand the effectiveness and success of marketing activities of an organisation. It consists of processes that measure, manage, optimise and analyse the performance of marketing activities. The objective is to improve effectiveness of marketing strategies and look into generating more profits in an organisation. The techniques used can help marketers and consumers. The marketing department can measure their marketing efforts and campaign effectiveness and optimise them. The consumers can view personalised advertisements as they convey information based on their specific interest. Marketing analytics helps organisations in making decisions on branding, product updates, improving sales, customer journey analysis. Marketing department analyses how customers respond with different email promotions and as per customer needs and expectations the messages are customised. Few advantages of marketing analytics are:

- Helps in trend predictions
- Helps stakeholders to have a holistic view of all marketing channels
- Improves lead generation
- Improves effectiveness of advertising
- Provides real time decision support
- Helps in better understanding of customer needs
- Creates better customer experiences
- Creates effective marketing strategy
- Validates advertising expenses
- Helps conduct competitor analysis

E.2. Financial Analytics

Financial analytics provides insights into the financial performance of an organisation. The applications capture finance and accounting data based on a company's historical financial transactions. This helps discover patterns and gain an understanding of the performance of the organisation. These patterns help the organisations predict and improve business performance and help in better decision making. Finance analytics are integrated with statistical analysis, financial modelling, and prediction. It helps gain in-depth knowledge and take strategic decisions for improving business performance. Few advantages of financial analytics are:

- Helps in efficient financial planning and forecasting
- Provides timely information for decision-making purposes
- Improves decision-making strategies to help attain the future goals of a business
- Helps in understanding the metrics and measures of a business
- Helps improving the business value by giving an in-depth insight into the organisation's financial status

E.3. Human Resource Analytics

Human Resource Analytics relates to people analytics with an objective to improve employee retention and performance. It does not focus on just gathering information on employees at work but gets insights on all the human resource processes. Analytics involves gathering data, getting insights and providing informed decisions. HR analytics is a methodology for creating insights on how investments in human resource assets in an organisation contributes to the success of four major outcomes: (a) generating revenue, (b) minimising expenses, (c) mitigating risks, and (d) executing strategic plans. This is done by applying statistical methods to integrate HR, talent management, financial, and operational data. Some of the advantages of HR Analytics are as follows:

- Helps identify the employees who would most likely to leave the organisation
- Helps identify patterns that get generated during employee turnover
- Helps estimate the amount of time taken to hire employees
- Helps measure employee performance after the learning and development initiatives
- Helps businesses make improvements and plan future initiatives

Data is gathered about employee profiles, performance data on high-performers, and low-performers, salary and promotion history, and demographic data. The data brings a process of continuous measurement and comparison, also known as HR metrics. HR analytics compares the collected data against historical norms and organisational standards. The process cannot rely on a single snapshot of data, but instead requires a continuous feed of data over time. The key metrics that are measured include organisation performance, its operations and process optimization.

The analytical stage reviews the results from metric reporting to identify trends and patterns that may have an organisational impact. There are different analytical methods used, depending on the outcome desired. Some of the well-known HR metrics include employee churn, absenteeism rate, engagement rating, and productivity. By measuring the metrics, predictive analytics is conducted by assessing the workforce turnover rate. These metrics also help understand the employee lifecycle from 'Hire to Fire' stage. Preventive measures can be taken once the prediction is conducted in an accurate manner.

E.4. Analytics in Manufacturing

Analytics is extensively being used in the manufacturing industry due to the advent of Industry 4.0 and the Industrial Internet of Things (IIoT). Essentially, digital transformation technologies and automation have ensured the availability of real-time production data in order to make decisions which are faster and better. Analytics in a production environment helps in planning, optimization, maintenance, quality management and improved efficiency. Traditional methods of data capture which are fragmented could be inaccurate due to human errors. Data collection could be filled with bias and time-consuming. This might lead to inaccurate decision making by managers. With the use of technology and utilisation of advanced analytics and algorithms, the insights derived would be real-time and accurate.

Some of the interesting use-cases in the application of analytics in manufacturing have added value to businesses in the recent past. Predictive maintenance application has improved exponentially due to the availability of real-time data from the production environment. Floor managers can least expect the unplanned break-downs leading to production loss. Due to prediction in the breakdown, technicians are able to perform repairs before the damage takes place. It is observed that deploying predictive maintenance and fault prediction mechanism, overall downtime of the machine comes down leading to better productivity.

Better inventory control is achieved through accurate demand forecasting. This also helps in the control of supply chain as demand planning is a complex exercise in the entire process flow. In a production environment, it is essential to estimate the spare parts requirement, duration of a process in a work-flow, cost associated with the same and the profit achieved. This understanding helps in the process of accurate forecasting. Organizations invest in Research & Development (R & D) in order to create new product lines, improvising of models which already exist or sun-set some of them so that they remain competitive in the market. Based on the inputs from R & D, product developments take place. Advanced manufacturing analytics strategies are deployed for simulating the production process using 'digital twins' and other similar methods. This has helped the industry overcome the time-consuming iterative models leading to better performance prediction and reduction of R & D costs for organizations.

Thus, manufacturing analytics empowers organization by leveraging the huge volume of real-time streaming data from the production environment. Advanced techniques like visualization and dashboards, machine learning algorithms lead to actionable insights for better decision making by managers. Process optimization has led to reduced cost and labour. With real-time insights available in inventory management, supply-demand planning revenues increase due to better customer satisfaction. Other benefits include reduced consumption of energy, following of safety protocols and improved quality and compliance towards processes as they are being monitored through data generation.

1.3 ANALYTICS AT SHOPPERS STOP

Shoppers stop is a large retailer of beauty and fashion brands. They collaborated with Accenture to bring about digital commerce transformation across various retail channels. Since 2020, Shoppers Stop worked on transformation of their omnichannel strategy. They have strengthened their digital platform using analytics. Real time data gets generated across the value chain that includes supply chain, customer experience right from sales to last mile delivery. The digital platform of shoppers stop provides a single view of customer and market insights which helps in faster decision making. The objective is to improve customer satisfaction and enhance revenue generation. The advanced user interface helps the customers to have a seamless experience in the complete shopping cycle which includes browse, search, order, and return.

Shoppers stop has transitioned itself into an omni channel retailer from a brick-and-mortar store. Customers are able to shop safely through its website and application. The retailer has used analytics to target promotions during specific festivals. With the help of analytics, they found working women shop most often in the middle of the day for which they designed special programs to attract them into its stores. Sameer Amte, MD, Accenture says that in order to stay competitive, retailers need to constantly innovate as there is constant change in shopper's expectations. Retailers need to create experiences that engage and delight the customers. Shoppers Stop has been transitioning from being a brick-and-mortar to an omnichannel retailer, empowering customers with its digital initiatives to ensure a seamless shopping experience. Customers can shop safely, and at their convenience through WhatsApp or the website.

F. DATA SOURCES

Organisations have been generating huge volumes of data in the recent past. This is due to technological advancements, proliferation of devices and availability of seamless, efficient networks. Most of the organisations connect with the consumers through the internet, apps and social media. Consumers are able to access this information using their smart devices due to ubiquitous internet connectivity and cost-effective data plans. This data democratisation has led to the generation of huge volumes of data. Apart from the structured data which is available in tabular format, it is observed that data in the form of images, videos and audios are also prevalent. Due to this fact, organisations are in possession of data which is indeed a gold mine of information which will help make meaningful decisions by managers.

Prior to the arrival of the Internet in 1990's, organisations stored the data in their local database and ERP systems. Data sources which made these systems were mostly from Digital devices, Barcode scanners, POS systems, RFID systems, Personal Digital assistants, Sensors and some of them even through manual mode. Managers were able to generate push or pull reports from these systems and use them for decision making. Some of the reports were periodic and some were exceptional and many were ad hoc depending upon the scenario. Most of these reports are structured in nature with standard rows and columns. Decisions were made based on data instead of being intuition based leading to rational decision-making processes.

Organisations which are more than four or five decades old, had their data storage, data processing done through EDP or MIS departments. Employees who had expertise in the technology field handled the data, generated reports and supported their business managers in the decision-making process. As organisations graduated towards ERP systems, where the entire organisation data is stored in a single repository, there was a need for the functional managers to be equipped with the technical aspects of running a business. In an ERP system, a repository is created by integrating the data from the various functional areas like Finance, Human Resources, Marketing, Manufacturing, Supply chain among others. Modules like Materials Management, Production Planning, Sales & Distribution, Customer Relationship Management evolved by integrating data across functional areas. This led to deriving insights which were not visible in the periodic reports improving the decision-making process. Better competitive advantage, improved market share, increased profits were achieved due to the improved decision making.

Organisations felt the need to generate more data, store them optimally and retrieve them in an efficient manner. The process of data generation is achieved through various technologies which evolved during the past three decades. ERP systems became more of a necessity than a luxury. Technology was adopted by every domain like retail, healthcare, automobile, airline, government, banking, insurance, entertainment and much more. Non-adopters were left alone in the race to achieve growth in organisations as the benefits achieved through technology adoption were measurable and scalable. Consumers had better access to products and services information through websites and applications. Technology adoption brought in transparency in transactions and data availability. This led to more consumers and citizens adopting technologies using smart devices. The aforementioned changes in the way information were gathered led to huge volumes of data generation across sources.

G. DATA QUALITY

As in any change, scalability brings its own challenges. Especially, with respect to data generation, it has gone through an exponential growth over the past three decades. If the insights to be derived are reliable and genuine, it is essential to monitor the data quality. The parameters to measure data quality are completeness, consistency, reliability and timeliness. In order to ensure data quality, it is important that the automated data collection process is streamlined while creating a user interface. Digitisation has ensured improved data quality as manual data entry errors are eliminated. As we know, if the data that goes in a system is of poor quality, the outcome would also be of the same nature.

Data could be incomplete if it is truncated without enough space to fill in the information in user interfaces. Similar data present across various platforms could be inconsistent and a good amount of data pre-processing or cleaning ensures consistency. Sources of data need to be reliable so that the insights derived help in the decision-making process. Data remains time critical and it loses its relevance if it is not available at the right moment.

H. DEALING WITH MISSING OR INCOMPLETE DATA

While collecting data through surveys, there are chances that the user may not have filled all the relevant columns. This leads to poor derivation of insights and further improper decision making. The cause of this situation could be due to user interfaces which are not checked and incomplete due to the optional columns given in the data collection process. There are techniques and tools which are available to deal with such a situation. Imputation of these values with the nearest data point is one of the methods. Deleting a row which has more missing values is another approach. Data being valuable, enough effort needs to be taken to ensure that relevant data is not missed out. As data loss leads to poor insights.

I. ROLE OF DATA SCIENTIST IN BUSINESS AND SOCIETY

From the discussions, we understand that analytics is the future of any sector. Professionals with these skill sets are most sought after in the industry. The capabilities will help businesses cut costs, improve market share, improve productivity and efficiency in businesses. Apart from this, analytics have helped solve problems related to traffic management, logistics, customer engagement and individuals too. For example, Google maps is an excellent application which could be used in a daily scenario by users. Data scientists are professionals who have analytical and problem-solving skills for the benefit of business and society. Businesses could have problems related to their growth and sustenance. Whereas, for the society applications need to be at the user level right from applications like Arokya Setu, e-Governance and UPI. There is no doubt that data scientists have a big role to play in changing the way businesses, government and society is run till the time relevant data is available for the purpose.

CONCLUSION

This chapter brings out the definition and concepts of analytics and its applications. This also highlighted the types of analytics namely - Descriptive, Diagnostics, Predictive and Prescriptive analytics in order to achieve business decisions using data. We observe that descriptive and diagnostic analytics focused on the past data whereas, predictive and prescriptive analytics focused on the future. Applications of analytics across various functional areas are discussed. Also, issues related to the quality of data and the relevance of data scientists as a change maker in business and society is elaborated.

POINTS TO BE REMEMBERED

In the recent past, Analytics has become a crucial part of business decision making. Irrespective of the domain and function, there are successful applications which have benefitted businesses in increasing profit, achieving competitive advantage and increasing market share. The process of analytics involves a step-by-step approach from Descriptive, Diagnostic, Predictive to Prescriptive. The key for a successful analytics solution is data which must be of good quality leading towards optimum solutions. This makes the role of a data scientist important while solving business problems.

KEYWORDS

Data	Data Quality
Descriptive Analytics	Finance Analytics
Diagnostic Analytics	Marketing Analytics
Predictive Analytics	Human Resources Analytics
Prescriptive Analytics	Analytics in Manufacturing
Data Sources	Missing Data
Applications of Analytics	Business Analytics

MULTIPLE CHOICE QUESTIONS

1. Data ___________ refers to the quality of data to be analysed.

   a. Velocity
   b. Veracity
   c. Variety
   d. Volume

2. _______________analytics is the process of transforming data into insights to improve business decisions.

   a. Risk
   b. Fraud
   c. Data
   d. Business

3. The Science of analyzing raw data to make conclusions about that information is

   a. Data merging
   b. Data Analytics
   c. Data Refining
   d. Data Cleansing

4. The business analytics technique that answers questions about what has happened is called

   a. Predictive analytics
   b. Diagnostic analytics
   c. Prescriptive analytics
   d. Descriptive analytics

5. To determine the likely future outcomes, wc use ___________ by building models based on historical data

   a. Prescriptive analytics
   b. Diagnostic analytics
   c. Predictive analytics
   d. Descriptive analytics

6. The business analytics technique that helps to understand why this happened is called ________________ analytics

    a. Prescriptive
    b. Predictive
    c. Diagnostics
    d. Descriptive

7. _____________________ to identify patterns and trends and extract usable data from the largest set of raw data.

    a. Data Cleansing
    b. Data Mining
    c. Data aggregation
    d. Data Integrity

8. The process of gathering data from multiple sources with the intention of creating a summary is

    a. Data Mining
    b. Data gathering
    c. Data aggregation
    d. Data Integrity

9. A part of descriptive analytics in which data is represented graphically using charts and various other techniques in order to help stakeholders identify trends and patterns is

    a. Data graphics
    b. Data gathering
    c. Data Visualization
    d. Data Integrity

10. Business analytics techniques that help to find answers to the question 'what should we do in the future' are called.

    a. Prescriptive analytics
    b. Data analytics
    c. What if analysis
    d. Descriptive analytics

Answers

1. b. **2.** d. **3.** b. **4.** d. **5.**c **6.** c. **7.** b. **8.** c **9.** c **10.** a

CONTENT QUESTIONS FOR DISCUSSION

1. What is the fundamental purpose of analytics and how does analytics help in contributing to informed decision making in various industries?
2. In what ways is analytics differing from traditional decision making and in what advantages does it bring in terms of accuracy and efficiency?
3. Define the four main types of analytics and give a brief example of each type
4. List and briefly explain some characteristics of analytics.
5. How does Business analytics help in strategic decisions?
6. Provide a list of software tools used in analytics and briefly describe the features
7. Why is analytics crucial in this age of digital transformation?
8. Explain why analytics can be considered as a crucial asset for fostering innovation.
9. Explain how analytics addresses the challenge of information overload in decision making
10. Explain the role of analytics in turning data into actionable insights for informed decision-making.
11. How can analytics help organizations stay competitive in rapidly evolving markets?
12. Define Business Analytics (BA) and distinguish it from other forms of analytics.
13. How has the rise of data availability influenced the prominence of analytics in today's business landscape?
14. How does analytics transform raw data into valuable insights for decision-making?
15. How has the rise of data availability influenced the prominence of analytics in today's business landscape?

EPILOGUE

The chapter introduced the concepts of analytics, the various types, its applications across functions and domains. Beyond this, it brought focus to the data sources and its quality in order to achieve effective and impactful business decision making.

CONNECT TO THE NEXT

Having got introduced to the concepts of analytics, the next chapter discusses about the methodology or the process involved the analysis. A step-by-step approach is adopted for a detailed understanding.

REFERENCES

https://www.thoughtspot.com/data-trends/business-analytics

https://intellipaat.com/blog/what-is-business-analytics/

https://www.datatobiz.com/blog/big-data-analytics-use-cases/

https://u-next.com/blogs/business-analytics/applications-of-business-analytics/

https://www.simplilearn.com/business-analytics-applications-and-use-cases-article

https://www.analyticssteps.com/blogs/real-world-applications-business-analytics

CHAPTER 02

Analytics Methodology

Tagline – "Steps to analyse data"

PROLOGUE

Analytics is the process to achieve an outcome which would help in businesses taking data driven decisions. It involves a step-by-step approach with clear objectives. It is essential for an analyst to follow this structured approach in order to ensure an ethical and responsible act of analysis using good quality data.

CHAPTER OUTLINE

A. INTRODUCTION TO ANALYTICS
B. METHODOLOGY
C. PREPARING OBJECTIVES
D. GATHERING DATA
E. DATA COLLECTION METHODOLOGY
F. DATA COLLECTION METHODS
G. ADVANTAGES AND DISADVANTAGES OF DATA COLLECTION METHODS
H. DATA COLLECTION METHODS USED IN BUSINESS ANALYTICS
I. DATA CLEANING
J. DATA INTERPRETATION
K. SHARING THE RESULTS

LEARNING OBJECTIVES

The objectives of this chapter are

- To encourage learners to have a clear objective before working on the analysis

- To introduce learners to the steps and processes towards conducting analysis
- To appreciate the value of data and its quality during the analysis stage

A. INTRODUCTION TO ANALYTICS

Business organisations survive on data generated through devices since the arrival of computing machines. It is impossible to make informed decisions without reliable data and information. Analysts look for high quality, accurate, efficient data to make impactful decisions. Data analysis is the process of gathering and processing raw data. Data thus gathered is cleansed and converted into useful and relevant information which helps businesses to make informed decisions. The data analysis methodology helps in reducing the apparent risks involved in decision-making. The outcomes are presented visually in the form of graphs and charts with the help of tools.

We can take a simple example from our daily lives when we make conscious decisions to avoid water wastage. The decision we make currently is based on the problems we faced in the past due to water scarcity. Basically, this process of analysing past experience, evaluating what happened in the past or what will happen in future is based on data analysis.

B. METHODOLOGY

It is recommended to adopt a step-by-step approach while working with data. Due to the deluge of data which is present across sources and the flood of tools offered by tech companies, it is natural that the analyst gets carried away to import the data into the tool and proceed with the analysis. However, it may not be a good idea to conduct analysis in an instant manner. The insights which are derived out of such analysis may not lead to an efficient data driven decision. It is possible that the decisions taken are not in sync with what the organization needs. Hence, there is a need to have a methodology or a process or a framework to be followed prior to the actual data analysis process.

C. PREPARING OBJECTIVES

The first step in data analysis is defining the objectives. The objectives are derived out of the problem statement one needs to address. One way to do this is to frame a hypothesis and plan a methodology to test the hypothesis. While doing this, certain questions emerge which involves determining business objective or business problem that is attempted to be resolved. Definition of the objective or stating the business problem is very crucial so that the problem solver heads towards the right direction for data analysis. For example, senior management team questions the marketing department on decline of sales of a product. If the issue of downfall of sales is to be resolved then the analyst has to comprehend the root cause of the issue by understanding the characteristics of the product. The analyst needs to also compare the performance of the current organization in terms of market share and popularity with that of the competitors.

D. GATHERING DATA

Once the objectives are defined, the analyst needs to work on data gathering and organizing the same in an appropriate format needed for analysis. In this case, data could be either quantitative or qualitative in nature. Data, in general can be classified into three types based on the sources.

- First-party data: Gathered directly from users by an organisation
- Second-party data: Shared by another organisation about their customers
- Third-party data: Gathered by third party organisations

Let us understand each category of these data types in detail:

D.1. First-party data

This data is gathered by the organisation or a user directly from the customers. The source of the data could be from customer relationship management system or transactional system. Few other examples of first-party data sources include -

- Customer feedback
- Social media (no of people following social media site, no of likes, comments, shares)
- Subscription data, customer reviews
- Lead forms (email address)
- Marketing automation software (lead score of prospective customers)

Such data is highly valuable for the organisation. This data would be of high volume, structured and easily analysable using a tool. Getting access to this data needs permissions and authentication as it is personal and confidential.

1.4 PEAK LEARNERS

Peak learners, a startup company is into development of customised training software for its customers. The firm is very comfortable acquiring new customers; however, retaining them seems to be a challenge. This situation raises questions about why the organisation does not get repeat orders from the customers and ponders into aspects dealing with customer experiences. Problem here could be the features of the product, poor user interface, lack of adoption by users among others. In this case once the problem is defined, we can look for data sources which will help understand the problem and resolve it. In order to achieve this, it is important to identify the right data sources.

The data sources to analyse the problem could be from the feedback received from the users through structured questionnaire or interviews conducted through semi-structured questionnaires. The results of the questionnaire can be analysed using various tools and techniques. This step of data analysis is not only related to usage of tools but it involves business knowledge, lateral thinking, application of soft skills among others. Tracking Key Performance Indicators (KPIs), business metrics can also be put into use while formulating a problem statement prior to solving a business problem. There is open-source software like Dash builder which can help build dashboards through visualization from start and end of data analysis process.

D.2. Second-party data

Second-party data includes the first-party data collected from other companies. The data is collected from the private marketplace or directly from the company. The sources can be similar to the data gathered in first-party data like customer reviews, social media, web logs, etc. This can be used for targeting new customers and gaining insights about their behaviour. The data from the second-party gives advantage of being dependable and structured. The advantage of second-party data is that it allows companies to access relevant data without collecting it directly from the source. Such type of data often comes at a cost through various agencies.

D.3. Third-party data

Third-party data is gathered and segregated using multiple sources through a third-party organisation. In this case, data gathered is mostly unstructured in nature. Data is collected from various companies and used for preparing industry reports, marketing research, different types of analytics in various functional areas. Data from third party organisation can be Government portals, open-source data from various company websites or repositories. For example, data available publicly on websites like censusindia.gov.in or india.gov.in about India's census data.

Examples include

- Purchase history of customers
- Demographic data like Name, phone numbers, email addresses, postal address
- Web browsing habits
- B2B data sold by companies that process, collate and resell the data from multiple sources like Dun & Bradstreet

E. DATA COLLECTION METHODOLOGY

Data collection is the method of gathering relevant data from a genuine source. This helps the user answer various queries and evaluate the results. The results help analyze the information obtained through proper methods so that the objectives are achieved. Data can be collected through various methods. One of them is Questionnaires and Surveys. A list of questions which are circulated amongst the target audience as a means to conduct a survey is a questionnaire. This can be open-ended or close-ended. Open-ended questions are often used for complex questions as they do not just gather answers. They look into more details and gives an opportunity for the interviewer to analyse the responses in detail.

Surveys are used to circulate a list of questions to a set of respondents. In some cases, it may not be just a set of questions, but a purposive data collection process at a macro level in a short duration. It can be administered online, over phone or in person. Customer surveys are done to gather data about customer satisfaction, product or service quality, and customer loyalty. When the organisation knows what the customers think and need, it can make plan and strategies activities which will lead to the customer satisfaction. As we observe here, surveys are outcome based adding value to the business through improved sales or increased market share.

1.5 ANALYTICS IN COCA-COLA

Coca Cola is an American multinational beverage corporation. It has its headquarters in Atlanta, Georgia. The company is serving the people of more than 200 countries across the globe, with more than 500 different brands ranging from Coca-Cola to Zico Coconut Water, to Costa coffee. Dr John Pemberton served the world›s first Coca Cola at Jacobs Pharmacy in Atlanta in the year 1886 and from an iconic drink they transformed into a complete beverage company. At present Coca Cola is serving more than 200 countries with 1.9 billion customers. They prefer various Coca Cola drinks like Coke, Fanta, Spirit, Costa Coffee and many more. A lot of data is generated within the organization on a daily basis which includes production details, customer details, customer feedback, sales data, sourcing data among others. Coca Cola uses bigdata for strategic decision making. Data Analytics helped them to understand the customers preferences and work out on formulation of new products as per the customer taste. Purchase behaviour, preference of flavours varies from region to region and analytics helped them to personalise the products region wise.

Coca Cola used observation and interview as means of data gathering. The interviews were through mail, face to face or taking an opinion poll through social media. Technologies like AI, ML, big data analytics helped them to grow and change the traditional methods of data gathering, marketing and understanding their customers. Coca Cola has a huge customer base. They used ML for product development, and improved personalization. They gathered data about customers who were using the vending machines, picking from stores and other areas. Using analytics, they understood the customers purchase patterns, their likes, and demands. The vending machines were stocked with appropriate products for a particular location and discounts were offered related to that specific unit. Based on the location, whether a person is in a gym, movie hall, jogging, the machine sets its 'mood'. Artificial Intelligence (AI) was used in target marketing. The company tapped the use of AI to identify pictures of its products that were uploaded on social media platforms and generated ads to individuals based on those images. This increased the effectiveness of targeted advertising by four times compared to other means of advertising.

F. DATA COLLECTION METHODS

F.1. Interviews

Interviews are a common means of gathering data. It involves asking people their views, opinions, experiences with a clear objective of the interview in mind. Interviews are conducted through face-to-face meetings, video conferencing or over phone through semi-structured questionnaire. The entire process can be recorded with the permission of the interviewee for further analysis. Identifying the right interviewee with the right set of questions is the key to the success of this data collection method.

F.2. Observations

Data is gathered by observing various events as they occur or by observing people. In certain situations, it is difficult to measure the outcome through surveys and interviews. In such cases observation method is adopted. An example is ethnography where the researcher stays and interacts with the group and observes their behaviour. The data such collected would be qualitative in nature.

F.3. Focus Groups

A focus group involves collecting opinions on a particular topic from a small group of people. Consumer behaviour or their perceptions are studied by interaction with focus groups. These groups are homogeneous with people of similar interest or experience. The responses solicited from these groups are generally qualitative in nature and further interpretation is needed through analysis.

Secondary Data

Secondary data is the data that has been collected already and is available in the form of studies, articles, open data portals, Government sources among others. It can help the researcher get an overview of a topic or find trends. Some of the data sources are available for free and many are paid. With the immense data growth in the recent past through digital devices, ownership of data has become a business model.

F.4. Oral Histories

Oral histories are a method for data collection, that records details about personal experiences which people share. It is done using an audio or video recording of people's interactions. It can be recordings of an event too. This is used in speech recognition and transcription of audio data.

In general, data collection methods can be broadly divided into two main categories: Quantitative and Qualitative methods.

Qualitative data contains non-numerical information and is descriptive in nature. It is used to understand view-points, and ideas. It allows analysts to understand an issue in depth. Quantitative data is numeric in nature and this is commonly used for measuring outcomes by testing hypotheses. Quantitative data is gathered using questionnaires, surveys and other methods.

G. ADVANTAGES AND DISADVANTAGES OF DATA COLLECTION METHODS

Now that we have seen the types of data collection methods, we can observe that each data collection method has its own advantages and disadvantages.

Advantages of quantitative data include:

- Providing in depth description of data items
- Providing context details
- Helping in framing hypothesis and testing
- Flexible
- Reliable

Advantages of qualitative data include:

- Easy to analyse
- Easier to compare
- Data availability across media platforms

H. DATA COLLECTION METHODS USED IN BUSINESS ANALYTICS

Based on the business problem, we select the data gathering method/s to solve the problem. The data is gathered based on how it is going to used, what we need to understand in our business and the type of data that is required. When we get answers to the questions, we can choose the best method to gather data. Some common methods that are used in business analytics to gather data include:

- Customer Surveys
- Focus Groups

- Website Analytics
- Customer Support Monitoring
- Audio and Speech Data Collection

Website analytics tools like Google Analytics gather data about user behaviour and website visits. It gives an idea how people perceive the company's website. This data can help in improving the website design and user experience.

Customer Support Monitoring

Social media data, customer service, automated help desk data are all part of customer support data. Data about industry, company, customers, brand is gathered through social media. One can use this data to track customer sentiment, understand what people say about a brand, or measure the success of marketing campaigns of an organization.

Audio and Speech Data Collection

In applications related to communication systems, speech recognition systems or audio and speech data is used. The data collected is recorded, and analysed, from the audio signals which are extracted from the source. There are several ways to collect audio and speech data, which includes manual transcription, automatic speech recognition, and telephone surveys. Audio signals can be transcribed by hand and this process is known as manual transcription. It is a time-consuming process, but it is accurate and can be used to collect data from any audio signal.

Automatic speech recognition (ASR) is faster than manual transcription, but it is not as accurate. ASR is an audio and speech data collection method that uses algorithms to transcribe audio signals automatically. When the analyst is clear about the data he needs for analysis and traces the sources, many tools are used. Examples of some software used include Salesforce DMP (data management platforms), Cloudera, SAS data management, and Snowflake.

A Data management platform (DMP) gathers, arranges and activates first-party, second-party, third-party user data from both online and offline sources. It even includes mobile platform sources. The data gathered is aggregated to build a detailed customer profile that drives for customisation / personalisation, and target marketing. DMP platform is like a storehouse of data containing ids of mobile devices, cookies and advertisement campaign data. The tool builds a customer database, segments it based on the demographic data, devices used, location, browsing habits

1.6 TACO BELL

Burman Hospitality is a Taco Bell's exclusive franchise partner in India. In a short span of time Taco Bell became India's most loved fast-food chain for Mexican food. They have over 50 outlets in India and are continuously scaling their operations. For data gathering Taco Bell uses professional interviewers by gathering and distributing self-administered surveys to customers. They feel this will avoid customers answering irrelevant questions and save their company's time.

I. DATA CLEANING

The data collected through various methodologies is prepared for further analysis to derive insights for efficient decision making in organisations. The process of data preparation involves data cleaning or data cleansing and data scrubbing due to which quality of data is ensured. Data cleaning is the process of identifying and rectifying (updating or deleting) incorrect, unwanted, irrelevant, outdated information from a database or a table. Data cleansing is performed interactively using scripting technique for batch processing or by using data wrangling tools. Batch scripts are run wherein instructions are stored as simple text files which contains lines with commands that get executed in sequence, one after the other.

In today's era of digital age, companies accumulate massive volume of data online. The raw data needs to be transformed to useful information. Useful information can be generated using statistical tools, web scrapping, visualisation tools. Data wrangling comes into picture when data is transformed to information. It is the process of converting raw data to a format that is easier to understand and comprehend. In data wrangling process data is cleansed, organised and structured in such a way that it is useful for data analysis and visualisation. Some data wrangling tools include

- Data wrangler
- Open Refine
- Google Data prep
- Excel Power query
- Skit

Essentially, data wrangling involves six steps which are as follows.

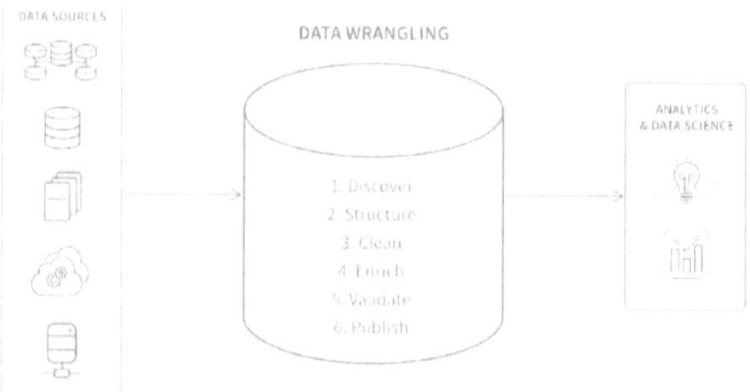

Figure 2: Data wrangling

Discovering: Prior to conducting data analysis, we need to understand the data. During discovering step, patterns in data or trends are identified, and issues like missing data, incomplete values are to be addressed.

Structuring: For analytical purpose data needs to be restructured. The data is segregated based on the criteria defined in the first step. Raw data is not usable in its raw state as it is not correctly formatted. It is either incomplete or not correctly formatted as per the requirements of the business. Data structuring is the process of taking raw data and transforming it in a format required by the analyst so that the interpretation is easier.

Cleaning: Data cleaning is the process of removing inherent errors in data that might distort the analysis or render it less valuable. Cleaning can come in different forms, including deleting empty cells or rows, removing outliers, and standardizing inputs. The goal of data cleaning is to ensure there are no errors (or as few as possible) that could influence the final analysis.

Enriching: By this step, users are familiar with the data set. Enriching can include adding context to data to get some sense out of the same. It may involve taking a step back and check if there is enough data to proceed ahead. It is not a good idea to proceed with data wrangling without having enough data as this will lead to missing out of important insights. If we want to launch a new product, we need lot of data regarding market conditions and customer preferences. The data needs to be strategized to get the right insight. The best method to get the refined data is to upscale or down sample it.

Validating: In validation step, we apply rules and analyse or evaluate the quality of data. Validation rules are applied repeatedly in sequence to check the consistency of data set. This will ensure the data quality and data security. After processing the data, the quality and consistency are verified that would establish a strong surface to the security issues.

Publishing: Data publishing is the final step in data wrangling. This can include providing documentation and notes of data wrangling process and give access or share with other users.

The insights obtained from the data wrangling process can be of immense value in future. Skipping this would result in poor data models that impact an organization's decision-making and reputation. Unfortunately, data wrangling is sometimes poorly understood, because of which its significance is overlooked. High-level decision-makers who prefer quick results may be surprised to see how long it takes to get data into a usable format. Unlike the results of data analysis (which often provides flashy and exciting insights), there is little to show for the efforts during the data wrangling phase. And as businesses face budget and time pressures, this makes a data wrangler's job all the more difficult. The job involves careful management of expectations, as well as technical know-how.

Let us discuss few scenarios where data wrangling is deployed.

Fraud Detection: Data wrangling can be applied to detect frauds in a company. This is done by capturing detailed information of web chats, multi layered emails and identification of unusual patterns/behaviour. Data security can be supported by providing the non-technical users to observe and wrangle data quickly to keep pace with multiple data security tasks. It also helps in improving compliances by aligning organisation procedures with Government and industry standards.

Customer Behaviour Analysis: Helps to quickly understand the business processes and gain insights about customers. Each customer is different, so the data collected about each customer also varies. Data wrangling helps to find similarities between customers for specific products or services and study the underlying patterns in them. This helps organizations gain an in-depth knowledge of the customer base.

Improved Reporting: In financial firms and other businesses, the various departments need to report their general results or some specific information frequently. When data that shows these results is raw and unstructured, it gets difficult to convey the correct information. In this situation data wrangling improves the quality of reports and ensures the management can get a correct understanding of information.

Unified Formats: In organisations, different departments use different systems to capture their data. Data wrangling consolidates the results of all branches in a single format unifying the data.

Data Quality: In an organisation, the data needs to be of a high quality to derive accurate insights from it. Every manager, analyst or executive focusses on getting high quality data. The various steps in data wrangling helps to derive a high-quality data.

Data cleaning: The process of recognising, replacing incorrect information, and/or replacing inconsistent or incorrect information from the database. In this process duplicate data items and irrelevant data are deleted. The standard data cleaning process consists of the following stages:

- Importing Data
- Merging data sets
- Filling missing data
- Data Standardization
- Data Normalization
- Deduplication
- Verification & enrichment
- Exporting data

Importing Data: When secondary data is used, importing data becomes straightforward. However, with primary data, this step is often underestimated.

Merging Data sets: Merging is combining two or more data sets to get information which is complete.

Filling Missing data: Missing data is the one that is not stored or present in the given dataset.

Data Standardisation: Data standardization is the process of converting data to a common format to enable users to process and analyse it.

Data Normalization: In order to conduct queries and analyze there is a need to reorganize data within a database. This helps in development of clean or good quality data. Redundant and unstructured data are thus eliminated and data appears to be more standardized.

Deduplication: The method of removing redundant data from the dataset.

Verification & enrichment: In this process, different types of data are checked for accuracy and inconsistencies. After treatment, the quality of data is enriched for further analysis.

Exporting data: Once the day is ready for analysis, the next step is to export the same from an Excel to any analytical tool which will help in conducting analysis to derive business insights.

Exploratory Analysis: In most of the scenarios exploratory analysis is done along with data cleansing. This helps in identifying initial trends and help reframing the hypothesis.

Data understanding is the knowledge that is gathered about the data, the needs that the data will satisfy, its content and location. The main two areas of data understanding are Data Assessment and Data Exploration.

Data Assessment

The first step in data understanding is Data Assessment. This should be undertaken before the start of the project since this checks the feasibility of the project. This task evaluates what data is available and how it aligns with the business problem. It should answer the following questions:

- What data is available?
- How much data is available?
- What is the format of the data?
- How the data can be accessed?
- Where is the data stored?
- Can data from multiple sources be merged?
- Which attributes are most important?
- What KPIs using this data should we focus on?
- What are the metrics obtained from this data?

One has to consider the data relevance, data quality, gathering the truth around ground data and being sensitive towards ethical practices of data during the collection and analysis process.

Data Exploration

Data can be explored once we have access to data. To understand the data, data summary can be prepared and the assumptions made in the data assessment stage can be tested. The questions to be answered here include:

- Is the number of records sufficient to conduct an analysis?
- What are the data types observed?
- Does it need to be changed as per the model designed?
- Are there missing values and how to handle them?
- Check for anomalies and outliers in the data set

To conclude, during the data exploration stage, the analyst needs to remove missing values, assess the outliers and ensure that the data is balanced in all aspects.

Data Ingestion

Data ingestion is the process of transmitting data from one or more sources to a place where it can be further processed and analysed. Data can be structured and unstructured from sources like databases, data lakes, and IoT devices.

Data Cleansing

Prior to the data analysis, the process of cleansing ensures that the outcome of the analysis is genuine. With ingested data it is possible to have multiple problems or challenges. These can be missing values, out of range values, and outliers. The analyst needs to cleanse the data thoroughly.

Format

Data needs to be formatted once it is cleansed. Data would have been gathered in different date formats, inconsistent naming conventions as per the wish and convenience of the person who collects data without relevant domain knowledge.

Combine

After cleansing and formatting the dataset, it is formatted by joining the data sets, merging or splitting the data. The data is transferred to data warehouse staging area after combining the data.

Data Normalisation

Database normalisation, or just normalisation as it is commonly called, is a process used where data is organised to reduce redundancy. The main objective of normalisation is to remove anomalies as these anomalies lead to redundancy. And in due course, this can lead to data integrity problems. Normalisation is the process which involves splitting relations (table) into well-structured relations to obtain a good database model that allows users to avoid redundancies in the tables and avoiding anomalies at update, delete and insert.

There are three types of anomalies:

- Insert anomaly
- Delete anomaly
- Update anomaly

Insert Anomaly: If a new row is inserted in a table and it creates the inconsistency in the table then it is called the insertion anomaly. For example, let us say we have a table that has four columns. Employee Id, Employee Name, Employee Address and Employee Performance. Now when a new employee joins, we can fill first three attributes but fourth attribute will have NULL value because he/she has still not started working and his/her performance is unknown.

Delete Anomaly: If we delete some rows from the table and if any other information or data which is required is also deleted from the database, this is called the deletion anomaly in the database. For example, let us say we have the information of the employee and projects he/she works on (employee deployed location, project id, project name). If any employee leaves the organisation, then the entry related to that employee will be deleted. However, deletion of the row will also delete the project information even though project depends upon the organisation and not the employee.

Update Anomaly: An update anomaly is a data inconsistency that results from data redundancy and a partial update. For example, if there are 20 columns out of which two are student name and student address. Now, if one student changes his/her place of stay then we would have to update the table. But the problem is, if the table is not normalized one student can have multiple entries and while updating all of those entries one of them might get missed.

In a database setup, there are a set of attribute/s that help us identify a row. These keys are also used when we want to establish relationships across various columns and tables of a relational database. Some of the keys are discussed here.

a) **Primary Key**: This key uniquely identifies each entry in a table. This value cannot be repeated within a table and cannot hold null values. Generally, first columns are defined as primary key. For example, Employee Id in Employee table.

b) **Foreign Key:** This key can have repetitive values, but to uniquely identify each entry the table can still have primary key column separate of foreign key column. However, the foreign key will create a relation with another table where those values are defined as primary keys.

c) **Composite Key**: This is the methods of defining multiple columns as primary key. Situations where no column have unique values in a table, we can define a combination of two or more than two columns as unique and set it as primary key. For example, in a student table - student name, address, marks, age, gender can be present as columns. Here, it is likely that multiple students can have same names. Therefore, we define combination of student name and address as primary key. Now it is unlikely that there can be student with same name and same address.

d) **Candidate Key**: In simple words, a candidate key is a key that can also serve as a primary key. For example, in a student table - student id, student roll no, address, marks are the columns. Here, student id is primary key because it does not have repetitive value and also there are no null values. However, student roll number holds all the properties of a primary key and thus considered as candidate key.

f) Surrogate Key: This means an artificially created value that uniquely identifies each entry in a table when no other column was able to hold properties of a primary key. It is an additional column and generally holds integer values.

Remember, we cannot make any changes to table which has its primary key work as foreign key in another table. In other words, we cannot make changes to a primary key if it is referred to by foreign key in from another table. Or to say, we cannot make changes to primary key of a parent table if it has a child with foreign key referring to parent's primary key.

Normalisation

Normalisation comprises of various types – 1NF, 2NF, and 3NF.

1NF: The first normal form signifies that each cell of the table must have a single value only. Therefore, the intersection of rows and columns must hold atomic values. For example, if we have a column name called phone number then each row for that column must save only single phone number.

2NF: We saw candidate key above and here is where it plays a role. 2NF rule signifies that no non-prime attributes in the table are dependent on any of the candidate key. In simple words, if the table is representative of two different entities, then it should be broken down into their own entities. For example, let us assume that we have a table by name student with columns student id, student name, course number, course name, teacher id, teacher name. This is essentially the information about each student enrolled in each course which is taught by each teacher in school. Since it is a representative of three different entities it must be normalized into 2NF form.

3NF: This rule signifies that tables must be in 2NF form and each table should only contain columns that are non-transitively depended on primary key of their own table. In simple words, if we have a table by name transaction with columns transaction id, price, quantity, and total sales then the total sales are found to be the product of price and quantity (price*quantity). Hence sales are transitively dependent in transaction id which is a primary key here. So, each attribute must directly depend upon the primary key.

Data blending is the process of combining data from multiple sources to create a single, new dataset. The dataset can be presented visually. It can be processed, analysed and used for business decisions. Data blending is different from data integration. In data blending process the data analyst or business analyst works on generating an analytic dataset which answers certain specific business questions. For example, database programmers use SQL join statements to blend data from different tables. Enterprises use datasets to answer a specific question or compare. It involves mashing up data from web analytics, spreadsheets., cloud etc. Data blending can speed up consumption of data. In data blending, there are two data sources; a primary data source and a secondary data source.

J. DATA INTERPRETATION

Once the data has been cleaned, we need to analyze. Based on the dataset and objectives we apply regression analysis, univariate/bivariate analysis.

Data analysis is basically categorised into 4 types of data analytics methods.

- Descriptive analytics
- Diagnostics Analytics
- Predictive Analytics
- Prescriptive Analytics

Descriptive Analytics: This type of analytics is when an analysis of data, which is mostly historical, is used to answer the basic question like "what happened?". It studies the events of the past and looks for specific patterns in the data. Commonly for descriptive analytics we use pie charts, bar charts, histograms and pivot tables. Visualizations commonly used for descriptive analytics include pie charts, bar charts, tables, or line graphs.

1.7 COCA-COLA USES DESCRIPTIVE ANALYTICS

Coca Cola, The Popular Beverage Company Uses Descriptive Analytics To Understand The Social Media Data Especially Twitter Where Discussions On Brand Takes Place. Consumers Tweet About Their Favourite Flavours, Government Taxes Etc. The Company Gets A Fair Amount Of Idea About

Consumer Likes And Preferences After Analysis Of Tweets. This Will Help The Company Take Informed Decisions.

Diagnostic Analytics: This type of analytics focusses on finding why a certain problem has taken place. Here the data is examined to answer the question, "Why did it happen?". It is characterized by techniques such as drill-down, data discovery, data mining, and correlations. For example, if the present sales report shows comparatively higher sales than average sales, the analyst can drill down on the internal sales data. This will help the company identify the reason whether this higher sale is due to new product or new features in the product. Or possibly, this could be due to a new segment of customers trying out the product. Some of the use cases are popularity of a new product in the market, sudden increase in the attrition rate in a particular sector, surge in the order of product in an online delivery platform among others.

1.8 COCA-COLA USES DIAGNOSTIC ANALYTICS

In the year 2003, an NGO in India CSE (Centre for Science and Environment) claimed that they have found out that the groundwater used in the Coca Cola bottling plant contained higher than the permissible pesticide levels. It contained carcinogenic compounds which could harm consumers. That reduced the sales of the Coca-Cola products by 11%, though later it was found the claims were false. Diagnostic analytics helped in understanding drop in sale. Quality is an important aspect of business that any serious company aimed at making profits should put into consideration.

Predictive analytics: This type of analytics is to forecast what will happen in the future with a high degree of certainty. This type of analysis helps to forecast future growth, detect future trends based on the data gathered before. Some of the use cases are prediction of churn in a telecom company, segmentation of customers, predictive maintenance in a manufacturing organization.

1.9 COCA-COLA USES PREDICTIVE ANALYTICS

Coca cola uses predictive analytics to find out which product will perform well in particular location. This information will help the company stock the required inventory and plan the supply chain for an effective delivery process. Sales prediction at the SKU level helps in the production as well inventory management. A right balance between demand and supply helps the company avoid over stocking and product non-availability scenarios.

Prescriptive Analytics:

This type of analytics helps its users make future recommendations in a business scenario. Being the final step in the analytics process, it includes all the previous steps that is conducted earlier. Retailers must be aware of the purchase pattern of customers who are their own and their competitors. This can be pulled out from search histories. Some of the use cases include the dynamic pricing strategies by airlines as the date of travel nears. This will help the airline maximize its profits given the uncertainty in the travel pattern due to weather, fuel costs and demand. As an example, when the system detects that pre-Diwali ticket sales from Bangalore to Delhi is less than the last year's, it automatically reduces the prices while ensuring that they are not far too low due to this year's higher oil prices.

1.10 COCA-COLA USES PRESCRIPTIVE ANALYTICS

Coca cola uses prescriptive analytics to suggest or recommend right pricing for the product. Based on the past purchases, and consumer behaviour, the company also ensures the positioning of the products in the right location for enhancement of sales. Due to supply-demand and seasonality aspect, there could be variation in the pricing and inventory. Both are managed with prescriptive analytics.

K. SHARING THE RESULTS

Sharing of the results with the stakeholders is the last step in analytics. Results are typically the insights derived from the data analysis. Various tools like dashboards, reports and other visualizations are used to share the findings and insights by the analyst.

CONCLUSION

This chapter brings out the definition and concepts of analytics and its applications. This also highlighted the types of analytics namely - Descriptive, Diagnostics, Predictive and Prescriptive analytics in order to achieve business decisions using data. We observe that descriptive and diagnostic analytics focused on the past data whereas, predictive and prescriptive analytics focused on the future. Applications of analytics across various functional areas are discussed. Also, issues related to the quality of data and the relevance of data scientists as a change maker in business and society is elaborated.

POINTS TO BE REMEMBERED

Prior to the commencement of the process of analysis, it is required to get the data ready by conducting various steps in order to achieve good data quality. The step-by-step approach will ensure an efficient data-driven decision-making process. Once the data preparation is completed, the data is ready for analysis again following the steps of Descriptive, Diagnostic, Predictive and Prescriptive analytics.

KEYWORDS

Data	Data Sources
Descriptive Analytics	Data Gathering
Diagnostic Analytics	Data Cleaning
Predictive Analytics	Data Normalization
Prescriptive Analytics	Data Quality
Methodology	Data Interpretation

MULTIPLE CHOICE QUESTIONS

1. The process of identifying and rectifying (updating or deleting) incorrect, unwanted, irrelevant, outdated information from a database, table is called

    a. Data collection

    b. Data collating

    c. Data volatility

    d. Data Cleansing

2. The process of transmitting data from one or more sources to a place where it can be further processed and analysed is

    a. Data ingestion

    b. Data Formatting

    c. Data volatility

    d. Data Cleansing

3. A process used where data is organised to reduce redundancy and anomalies is

    a. Data deletion

    b. Ingestion

    c. Normalization

    d. Data management

4. A key that uniquely identify each entry in a table. This value cannot be repeated inside a table and cannot hold null values is

    a. Secondary key

    b. Foreign Key

    c. Super key

    d. Primary Key

5. An artificially created value that uniquely identify each entry in a table when no other column was able to hold properties of a primary key is a

    a. Surrogate key

    b. Foreign Key

    c. Super key

    d. Primary Key

6. If a new row is added in a table and it creates the inconsistency in the table then it is called the

    a. Delete Anomaly
    b. Insert Anomaly
    c. Update Anomaly
    d. None of the above

7. In following step, we apply rules and analyse or evaluate the quality of data

    a. Data enrichment
    b. Data Publication
    c. Validating data
    d. Structuring data

8. A _______________ involves collecting opinions on a particular topic from a small group of people.

    a. Observation
    b. Focus Group
    c. Surveys
    d. Questionnaire

9. An example of a web site analytics tool is

    a. Crawler
    b. Google analytics
    c. Yahoo Search
    d. All the above

10. The data is gathered by the organisation or a user directly from the customers.

    a. Third party data
    b. No party data
    c. Second party data
    d. d. First party data

Answers

1. d. **2.** a. **3.** c. **4.** d. **5.** a. **6.** b. **7.** c. **8.** b. **9.** b. **10.** d.

CONTENT QUESTIONS FOR DISCUSSION

1. Define analytics methodology and explain its role in guiding the process of deriving insights from data.
2. How does a structured analytics methodology contribute to the efficiency and effectiveness of data analysis projects?
3. Give an outline of the key steps involved in identifying data requirements for an analytics project.
4. Why is it essential to have a clear understanding of data requirements for the success of subsequent data analysis phases?
5. Discuss the challenges associated with data collection and how these challenges can impact the quality of insights derived from the data.
6. Provide examples of different sources from which data can be collected for analytics purposes.
7. Explain the significance of data understanding in the analytics process and how it lays the foundation for meaningful analysis.
8. Describe the importance of data cleansing in the data preparation phase and provide examples of common data quality issues.
9. What are some potential consequences of neglecting data cleansing in the analytics process?
10. Define data normalization and elucidate its role in preparing data for analysis.
11. Explain the concept of data blending and its relevance in situations where data comes from multiple sources.
12. What challenges might arise when blending data from diverse sources, and how can these challenges be addressed?
13. Describe the process of data modelling and its importance in transforming raw data into actionable insights.
14. How can exploratory data analysis help in gaining insights into the characteristics and patterns within the dataset?
15. How does data modeling contribute to the extraction of insights from a complex dataset?

EPILOGUE

The chapter discussed about the various types of analytics, process involved in conducting a data analytics project and the issues plaguing data quality.

CONNECT TO THE NEXT

Having got introduced to the steps related to data analysis, the next chapter discusses about the summarization of data effectively and its process of visualizing data effectively in order to conduct an exploratory data analysis.

REFERENCES

https://careerfoundry.com/en/blog/data-analytics/data-analysis-techniques/

https://monkeylearn.com/data-analysis/

https://lpsonline.sas.upenn.edu/features/5-key-reasons-why-data-analytics-important-business

https://www.claravine.com/celebrating-second-party-data/

https://eecs.csuohio.edu/~sschung/cis611/ENACh10-Normalization-Modified_Chap15.pdf

CHAPTER 03

Visualization of Data

Tagline – "Represent data visually"

PROLOGUE

Data is typically a collection of numbers, text, labels in a specific context. Data collection may leave the data scattered without any structure thus meaning nothing to the end user. Data which is summarized, organized based on the text in a logical manner and represented visually leads to better data driven decision making.

CHAPTER OUTLINE

- A. INTRODUCTION
- B. DATA SUMMARIZATION METHODS
- C. TABLES
- D. CHARTS
- E. TYPE OF CHARTS

LEARNING OBJECTIVES

The objectives of this chapter are

- To summarize and organize data in a logical manner
- To visualize data using various plots
- To understand the distributions for better decision making

A. INTRODUCTION

Today's world is drowning in the ocean of data which are structured, unstructured and semi-structured in audio, video, text, tabular formats. The speed at which the data gets transferred is unimaginable as every one millionth of a second it takes place. This data explosion is due to the increasing size of internet users, web searches, smart devices, social media etc. It is estimated that there would be around 50 billion connected smart devices by the year 2030. Data is a valuable resource for every business across the sectors. Organizations across various sectors like banking, retail, food, railways, airlines are eager to leverage the data generated through applications and devices in order to build strategies for their organizations. It is a challenging task to analyze large volumes of data which streams real time into the organizations through devices. Data summarization and visualization seem to be useful as they provide crisp, insightful and comprehensive data summary to help organizations identify the existing opportunities and devise business strategies accordingly.

In common parlance, data is a collection of discrete or continuous variables that convey information in a specific context. It may describe the quantity, quality or facts in a simple interpretable format. Data can also be termed as something which can be translated to a form that is easier for processing for meaningful outcomes. Data can be collected by observations, measurements, survey or research. During this process, the collected data could be scattered or disorganized making the analysis process difficult and time consuming. Hence, there is a need to organize data in a logical manner by bringing structure to enable smooth analysis. Data organization helps one to categorize and classify data in order to make it more usable. A good data organization process helps organizations to get relevant insights and plays a major role in a company's success. Organized data leads to minimum errors with more accuracy, better efficiency as it saves cost, and let the researcher tell a better story.

Data Visualization is a technique which helps researchers represent data visually. These representations help in detecting outliers, identifying trends and clusters, spotting patterns and presenting results. Exploratory data analysis techniques enable better data quality and help analysts check the quality of data and enables the researchers to familiarize themselves with the structure of data. This technique helps a researcher tell stories by curating data into a format that is easier to understand, highlighting the trends and outliers. A good visualization must be able to tell a story, by removing the noise and highlighting useful information. Goal definition, data collection, data cleaning, identifying the right visuals and presenting the same in a simple, understandable manner are few of the steps to be followed for an effective data visualization.

B. DATA SUMMARIZATION METHODS

Data summarization is an important skill in business analytics. It is typically numerical or visual or a combination of these two aspects. It is considered to be part of exploratory data analysis. It is a science as it helps convey information effectively and it is an art as it explores the creative side of the presenter. The crispier the representation, better would be the insights which leads to effective decision making. The process is meticulously performed in a logical fashion so that the summary divulges significant patterns and trends in a transparent manner. It is also one of the initial steps in the data mining process which helps the researcher choose the statistical tool or technique based on the trends observed during summarization. Some of the prominent examples to help one understand the concept would be:

- A retail store manager would like to find out the sales performance of a health care product across various regions and demographics.
- An ecommerce company would like to find out the locations from where more orders are coming on in order to plan the delivery routes and personnel.
- An OTT platform would like to find out which genre of movies are most watched based on the age group, language etc.

Depending upon the statistical operations, there are three ways to summarize data.

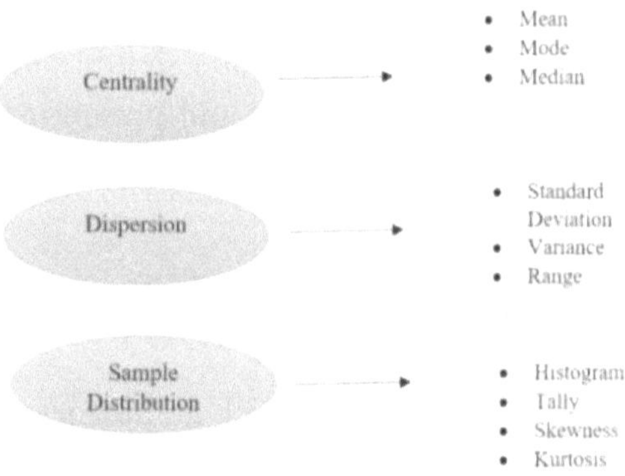

Figure 3: Types of Data Summarization

B.1. CENTRALITY

Once the numerical data is collected, it is organized in a logical manner. Centrality would be the centre of the middle value of a data set around which all other values of a data set revolve. This is otherwise known as 'average'. It is possible to summarize data based on centrality. Though there are multiple ways to find the centrality of data, the most commonly used methods are mean, mode and median.

Mean:

Common man generally uses the word 'average' in a casual manner, it usually refers to the mean. The mean of a set of numbers is arrived at by adding up all the numbers in the set and then dividing the result by the number of items in the set. It is generally used to calculate the numerical average of a dataset. For example,

The height in cm of people standing in a queue to pay bills in a Government office are given hereby:

152, 143, 144, 163, 154, 139, 150, 160, 172, 123.

In order to find the mean, we have to add all the items (x) in the dataset and divide the total by the number of items.

Mathematically this can be represented with a formula. $Y = \Sigma x/n$

Here, 'Σ' represents 'summation'; 'n' represents 'number of items'; Y represents the mean.

Solution: **Y = 1500/10 = 150**

So, the mean height in cm of people standing in the queue is **150 cm.**

Median:

Median refers to the middle value of the series when arranged in ascending or descending order. One can observe the tendency of mean and median to be same when the distribution is normal.

In order to find the median of a series in which the items are even in number, the mean of the two middle values is considered as the median. Whereas, if the items are odd in number, the middle item is considered as the median. The above steps are considered only when the series is organizing in ascending or descending order.

The marks of 12 students from a class in the subject English out of 100 are as follows:

46, 60, 72, 68, 74, 82, 52, 48, 62, 86, 90, 82

Median would be arrived at by organizing the items in ascending order as follows:

46, 48, 52, 60, 62, 68, 72, 74, 82, 82, 86, 90

It is observed from the above data series that the number of items is even. Hence, we would take the middle two numbers and their mean. This would be the median of this data series.

Median = (68+72) / 2 = 70

The median marks of the 12 students would be 70.

Median is preferred over mean typically in pay packets of employees in an organization.

Mode:

Mode indicates the value which occurs the greatest number of times in a data series. It can also be referred to as the most frequent number of the given dataset. Mode is generally used when the sample size is large or in cases where the data series are integers.

Consider the following marks of 10 students in a class out of 15.

15, 12, 13, 11, 12, 14, 9, 12, 11, 12.

It is observed that the most occurring marks is 12. So, we consider 12 as the mode of this data series.

B.2. DISPERSION

We just observed the data series from centrality perspective. Dispersion is a way of observing how the data is scattered around the mean. Within a given data, dispersion shows the presence of variability. Data points can be scattered away from the mean or could be closer to the mean.

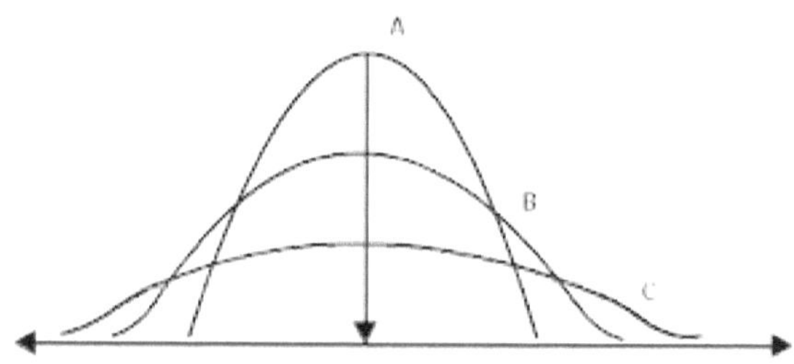

Figure 4: Measures of dispersion

In general, dispersion of a distribution is measured using variance and standard deviation. These are measured around a central value. Dispersion is classified into absolute and relative measures of dispersion. The most commonly used measure is standard deviation to understand the data spread. When the distributions are normal, data summarization can be optimally done with mean and standard deviation.

Variance

Variance is a measure of dispersion. This is statistical measure that is used to determine the spread of numbers in a data set with respect to the mean. We can arrive at the value of variance by taking the square of variance. This can be of two types – Population variance and Sample variance.

Considering a set of data group where all the members are known as the population. We can use population variance if we want to figure out how each data point in a given population is spread out. In cases where the size of the population is too large, it becomes difficult to take each data point into consideration. Here, few data points are picked up from the population to form a sample. This sample can describe the entire group. We calculate the variance always with respect to the sample mean.

Range

Range is a simple measure as compared to others but significant. It is the difference between the highest and lowest value of the data. It assists one understand the spread of data.

Figure 5: Range

Range = Highest Value - Lowest Value

For example,

To understand the monthly salary distribution in thousands of rupees among 8 employees in an organization, we can use range.

54, 42, 98, 12, 45, 52, 69, 71

Highest value = 98

Lowest value = 12

Hence, range is 98 – 12 = 86

B.3. SAMPLE DISTRIBUTION

This is a probability distribution of a statistics which is arrived at from choosing random samples of a given population. This is also known as finite-sample distribution. Typically, sample distribution depends upon multiple factors – the statistic, sample size, process of sampling and the population. The significance of sampling distribution lies in the fact that populations are typically large in size and randomly picking a subset needs a logic. This method eliminates variability and makes data to be managed in an easy manner.

Central Limit Theorem

It is a good idea to understand the central limit theorem as it helps in the construction of the sampling distribution of the mean. The theorem is based on the thought how the shape of the sampling distribution could be normalized as and when the sample size increases. As we plot the data, we would get closer to the shape of a bell curve.

Histogram

Histogram is a tool to visualize data and making it easier to understand. It is a graph with vertical columns that represent the frequency of a data point or range of data points occurring in a set of data. Histograms depict how many of a certain type of variable occur within a specific range. Typically generated out of a single continuous variable, it demonstrates the spread in a pictorial manner. Histograms are flexible and can be customized as per the need of the researcher. The interval buckets can be custom-made as per the need of the business problem.

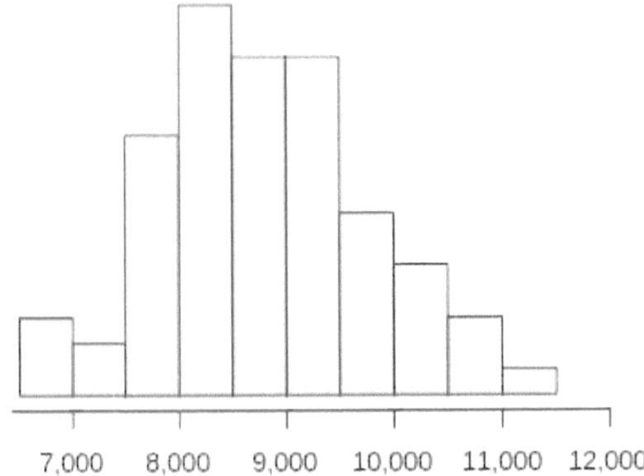

Figure 6: Histogram example – Salary range of six employees

Skewness

This statistical measure describes the lack of symmetry or asymmetry in the probability distribution of a dataset. Skewness is considered very significant in statistics as it gives insight into the nature of the distribution of a dataset. The measure has the ability to quantify the degree to which the data deviates from a symmetrical distribution which is bell-shaped. In critical applications related to the fields of economics and finance skewness plays an important role. Because to conduct analysis, the understanding of whether the dataset is positively or negatively skewed helps in better data understanding.

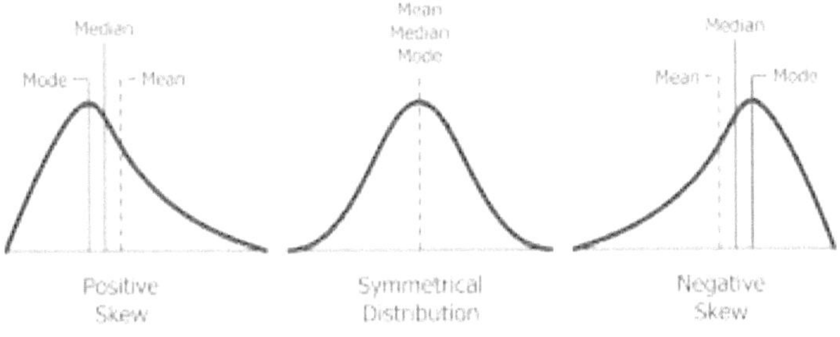

Figure 7: Skewness

Kurtosis

The data plotted in a graph takes the shape of a bell curve if it is normally distributed. This data which is away from the mean becomes the tail of the bell curve. The measure kurtosis defines how the data resides at the tails of the distribution. It identifies whether tails could contain extreme values. In other words, it describes the 'fatness' of the tails found in probability distributions.

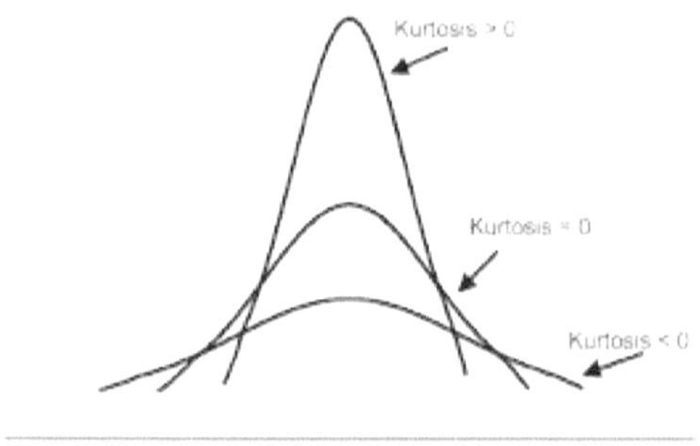

Figure 8: Kurtosis

C. TABLES

Tables are an effective way to represent data in a clear, concise and structured format.

While creating a table following steps can be observed. There needs to be purpose while creating a table and the researcher has to understand the message or aspect of what to convey.

It is essential to focus on the key variables or relationships which the table intends to project.

1. The table needs to have a set of columns and rows.

    Columns could represent categories or variables (e.g., Name, Age, Sales) and Rows can represent individual observations or data points (e.g., individual names, items, or time periods) and Headers must include descriptive headers for each column to explain the content.

2. Data needs to be sorted and organized logically in a table. It could be in alphabetical order for text, ascending/descending for numerical values and chronological order for dates. If required, data can be grouped for better explainability. Each column or row must indicate the units (e.g., Price (USD), Distance (miles))

3. It is essential to be consistent with fonts and spacing. It is a good practice to left align for better readability. With regard to numerical data, right again or center align is recommended. Applying borders and shading sparingly enhances the presentation of the table.

Name	Age	Occupation
Raghu	25	Engineer
Vani	30	Teacher
Pratibha	35	Designer

Year	Revenue (USD)	Expenses (USD)	Profit (USD)
2021	100,000	60,000	40,000
2022	120,000	70,000	50,000

Figure 9: Tabular representation

D. CHARTS

Charts play a vital role in analytics because they assist data to be represented in a visual manner. This makes it easier to interpret, analyze, and communicate complex information. Charts can add value to the way data can be explored, analyzed and interpreted. Here are some of the key ways in which this can be accomplished.

a. Charts simplify the data understanding

Charts have the capability to transform raw data into an easily digestible format by summarizin3g complex datasets into visual patterns, trends and relationships. The visual representations highlight insights that might not be observed immediately from numerical data.

b. Charts help identify trends and patterns
Charts like time series reveal trends over time (e.g., sales growth, stock prices). Scatter plots expose correlations or outliers within datasets.

c. Charts enhance decision making
Decision-makers can quickly grasp critical information through charts, leading to faster and more informed actions. Visual comparisons between datasets (e.g., bar charts for revenue comparisons) provide clarity in evaluating options.

d. Charts facilitate communication
Charts make it easier to present findings to stakeholders, by reducing dependence on jargon or technical explanations. They serve as universal tools for storytelling with data, bridging gaps between analytics teams and business units.

e. Charts help uncover hidden insights
Some relationships between data, like distributions or clusters are challenging to observe in a tabular format. But it becomes quite obvious in visual formats like histograms or heatmaps.

f. Charts help improve engagement
Visual representations are more engaging than rows of numbers or static reports, encouraging users to explore data actively. Interactive charts provide hands-on experiences that drive deeper engagement with analytics.

E. TYPE OF CHARTS

Common Types of Charts and Their Uses

- Bar Charts: Comparing quantities across categories.
- Line Charts: Analyzing trends over time.
- Pie Charts: Representing proportions or percentages.
- Scatter Plots: Identifying relationships and correlations.

- Heatmaps: Visualizing intensity or density within a dataset.
- Box Plots: Summarizing data distributions.

E.1. BAR CHARTS

Definition:

A **bar chart** is a graphical representation of data using rectangular bars, where the length or height of each bar is proportional to the value it represents. It is used to compare quantities across categories or track changes over time.

Types of Bar Charts:

1. Vertical Bar Chart:

- ○ Bars are displayed vertically, with the height of each bar representing the value.
- ○ Typically used when the categories are limited and the focus is on quantitative differences.

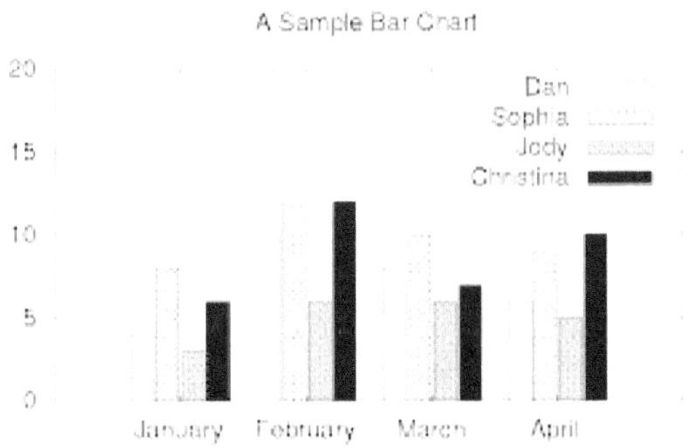

Figure 10: Vertical Bar Chart

2. Horizontal Bar Chart:

- ○ Bars are displayed horizontally, making it useful when category names are lengthy or there are numerous categories.

Figure 11: Horizontal Bar Chart

3. **Grouped Bar Chart:**

o   Multiple bars grouped together for each category to compare multiple data sets side-by-side.

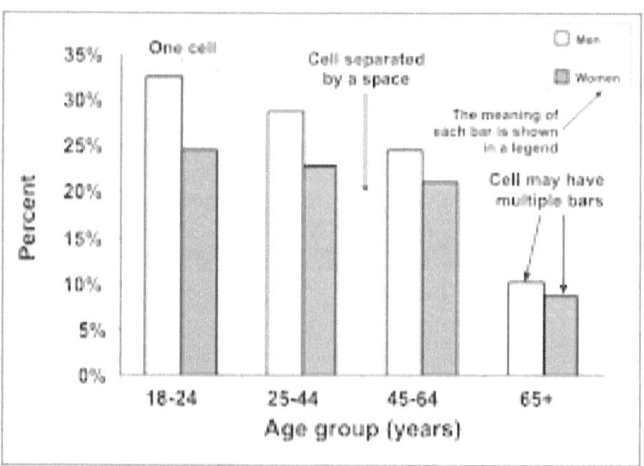

Figure 12: Grouped Bar Chart

4. **Stacked Bar Chart:**

o   Bars are divided into segments to represent parts of a whole. Each segment is color-coded for easy identification.

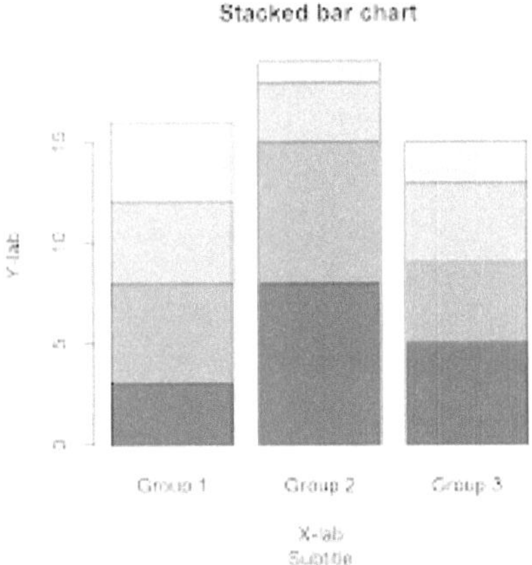

Figure 13: Stacked Bar Chart:

5. 100% Stacked Bar Chart:

○   Similar to a stacked bar chart, but the bars represent percentages, showing the proportion of each segment relative to the total.

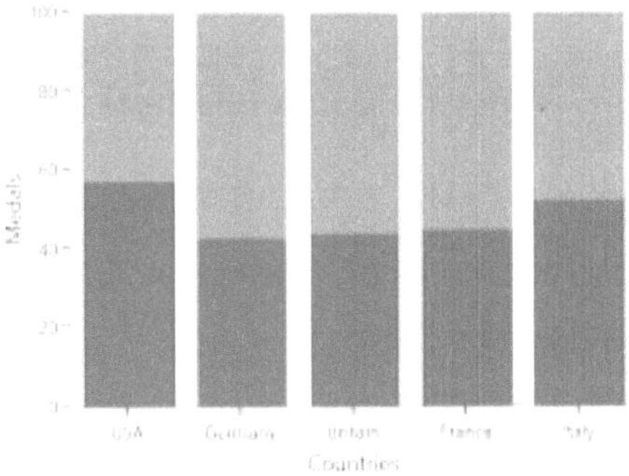

Figure 14: 100% Stacked Bar Chart

Uses of Bar Charts:

- **Comparison:** Comparing values across categories (e.g., sales across regions).
- **Trend Analysis:** Showing changes in data over time.
- **Distribution:** Visualizing frequency or distribution of data categories.

E.2. LINE CHARTS

A **line chart** is a type of graph that displays data points connected by straight line segments. It is commonly used to show trends, patterns, or changes over time by representing continuous data.

Types of Line Charts:

1. **Simple Line Chart:**

   - Displays one data set with points connected by a single line.
   - Useful for analyzing trends over time for a single variable.

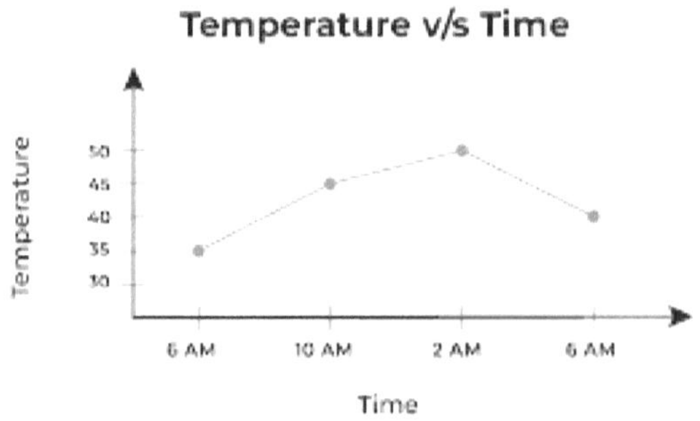

Figure 15: Simple Line Chart

2. **Multiple Line Chart:**

   - Shows multiple data sets on the same axes, with each data set represented by a separate line.
   - Useful for comparing trends across different categories or groups.

Figure 16: Multiple Line Chart

3. **Area Line Chart:**

- The area under the line is filled with color to emphasize the magnitude of values.
- Useful for emphasizing total trends or proportions.

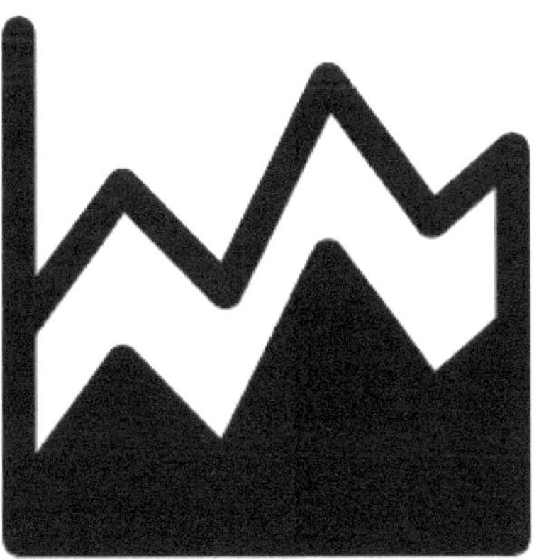

Figure 17: Area Line Chart

Uses of Line Charts:

- **Trend Analysis:** To track changes over time (e.g., sales, stock prices, temperature).
- **Comparisons:** Comparing multiple trends in the same time frame (e.g., revenue for different products).
- **Forecasting:** To predict future trends based on past data.
- **Visualizing Patterns:** Identifying recurring patterns or fluctuations.

E.3. PIE CHARTS

A **pie chart** is a circular statistical diagram divided into slices to represent proportions or percentages of a whole. Each slice corresponds to a category, and its size is proportional to the quantity it represents. It is best used for displaying parts of a whole.

Types of Pie Charts:

1. Simple Pie Chart:

- ○ The standard pie chart where each slice represents a single category.

Figure 18: Simple Pie Chart

2. Exploded Pie Chart:

- ○ A variation where one or more slices are separated from the rest of the chart to highlight specific data points.

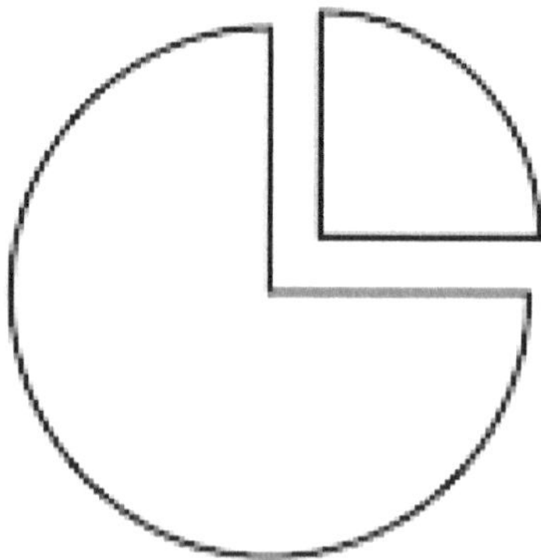

Figure 19: Exploded Pie Chart

3. **3D Pie Chart:**

- ○ Adds a three-dimensional effect for aesthetic appeal, though it can sometimes distort perception of proportions.

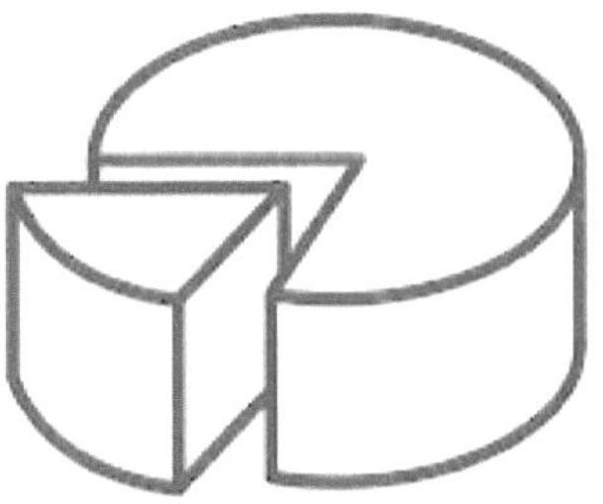

Figure 20: 3D Pie Chart

4. **Doughnut Chart:**

- ○ A circular chart with a hole in the center, offering a similar representation to a pie chart but with space for additional labels or graphics in the center.

Figure 21: Doughnut Chart

Uses of Pie Charts:

- **Proportional Representation:** Showing how individual parts contribute to the whole (e.g., market share, budget distribution).
- **Comparison:** Highlighting differences between categories in terms of proportion.
- **Data Simplification:** Providing a quick and visually appealing way to summarize data.

E.4. SCATTER PLOTS

A **scatter plot** (or scatter diagram) is a graphical representation of data points on a two-dimensional plane, where each point represents the values of two variables. It is used to identify relationships, patterns, and correlations between these variables.

Types of Scatter Plots:

1. **Simple Scatter Plot:**
   o Displays a single set of data points to examine relationships between two variables.

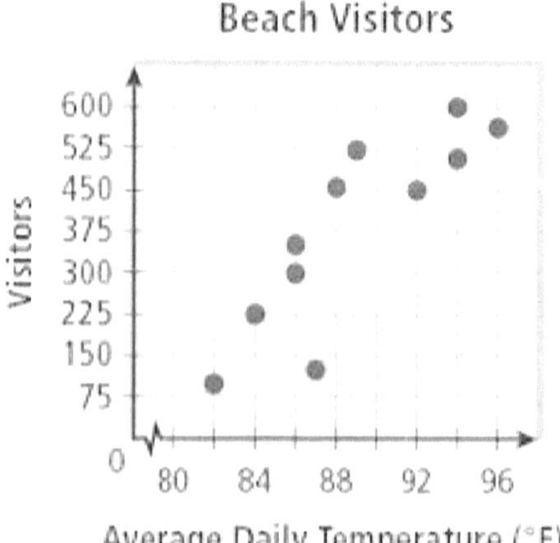

Figure 22: Simple Scatter Plot

2. **Grouped Scatter Plot:**

○   Groups data points into different categories, often distinguished by colors or symbols.

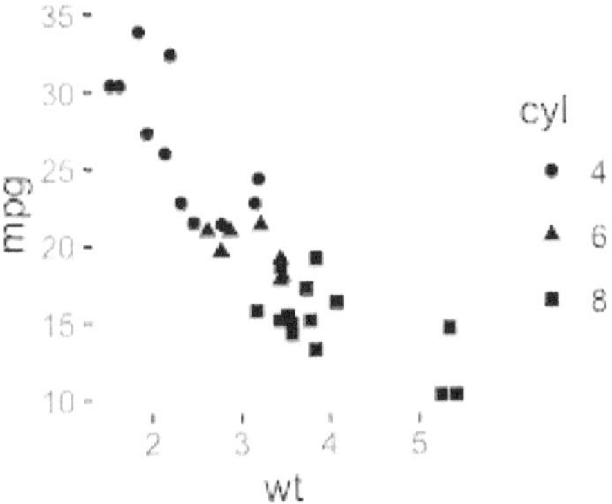

Figure 23: Grouped Scatter Plot

3. **Bubble Scatter Plot:**

○   Enhances the scatter plot by adding a third variable, where the size of the bubble represents the magnitude of the third variable.

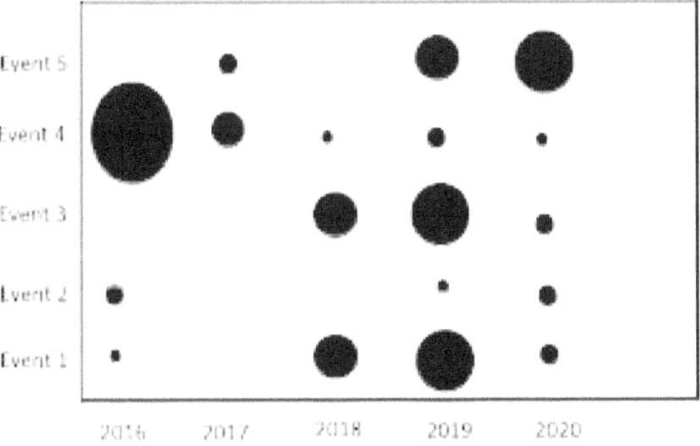

Figure 24: Bubble Scatter Plot

3 3D Scatter Plot:

- ○ Extends the concept to three dimensions, with each point positioned using three variables.

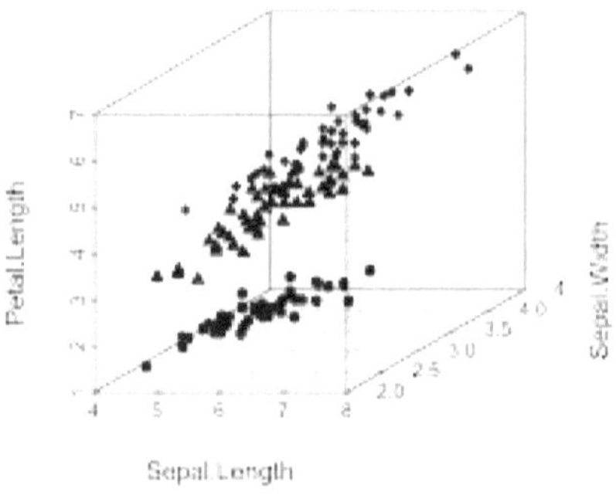

Figure 25: 3D Scatter Plot

Uses of Scatter Plots:

- **Correlation Analysis:** Identifying the type (positive, negative, or none) and strength of the relationship between two variables.
- **Outlier Detection:** Highlighting unusual data points that do not fit the overall trend.
- **Trend Identification:** Spotting patterns or clusters in data (e.g., linear, non-linear).
- **Cause-and-Effect Analysis:** Investigating dependencies between variables (e.g., study hours vs. test scores).
- **Visualization of Multivariate Data:** Using bubble or 3D scatter plots to represent more than two variables.

E.5. HEAT MAPS

A **heat map** is a data visualization technique that uses colors to represent the intensity, magnitude, or frequency of values within a dataset. It provides a quick and intuitive way to identify patterns, trends, or variations in data.

Types of Heat Maps:

1. Matrix Heat Map:

- Displays data in a grid format, where rows and columns represent variables, and the color intensity reflects the data values.

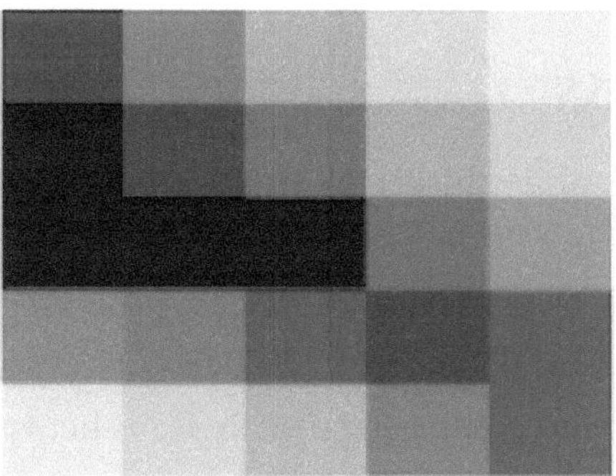

Figure 26: Matrix Heat Map

2. Geographical Heat Map:

- Overlays data on a map to highlight variations by location (e.g., population density, weather patterns).

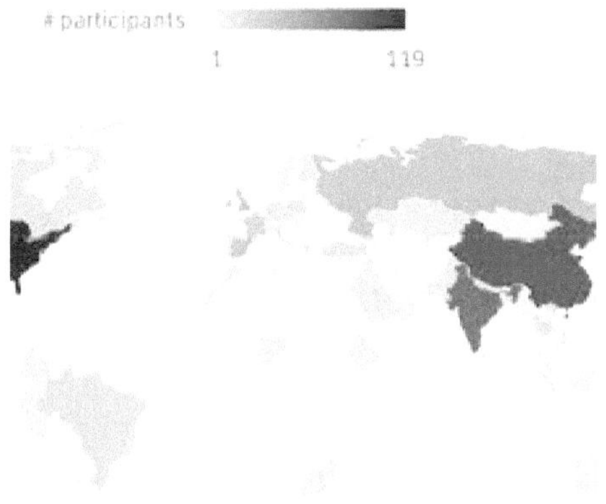

Figure 27: Geographical Heat Map

Uses of Heat Maps:

- **Pattern Recognition:** Spotting trends, correlations, or anomalies in data.
- **Comparison:** Comparing different categories, time periods, or geographical regions.

E.6. BOX PLOTS

A **box plot** (or box-and-whisker plot) is a graphical representation of the distribution of a dataset. It shows the minimum, first quartile (Q1), median, third quartile (Q3), and maximum values, providing a summary of the data's spread and central tendency. Box plots are particularly useful for identifying outliers and comparing distributions between groups.

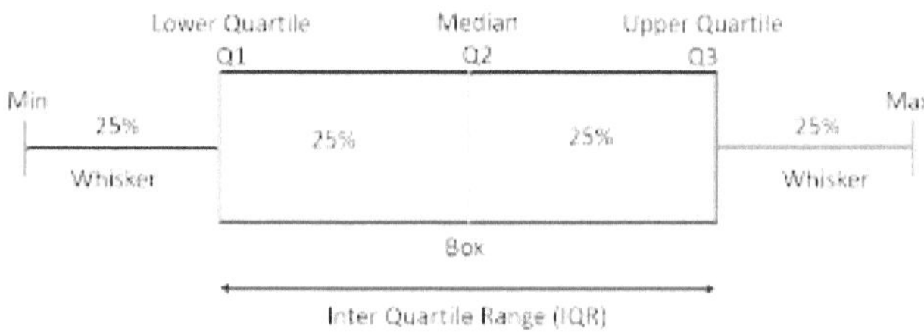

Figure 28: Box Plot

Types of Box Plots:

1. Standard Box Plot:

- Displays a single dataset using a box for the interquartile range (IQR) and whiskers for the minimum and maximum values.

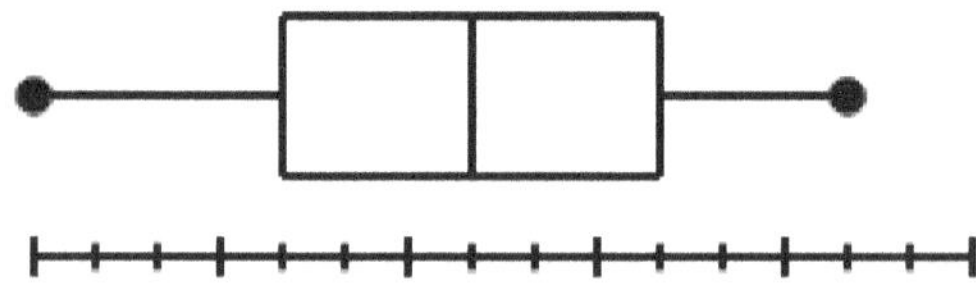

Figure 29: Standard Box Plot

2. **Grouped Box Plot:**

- ○   Multiple box plots are arranged side by side to compare distributions across different categories or groups.

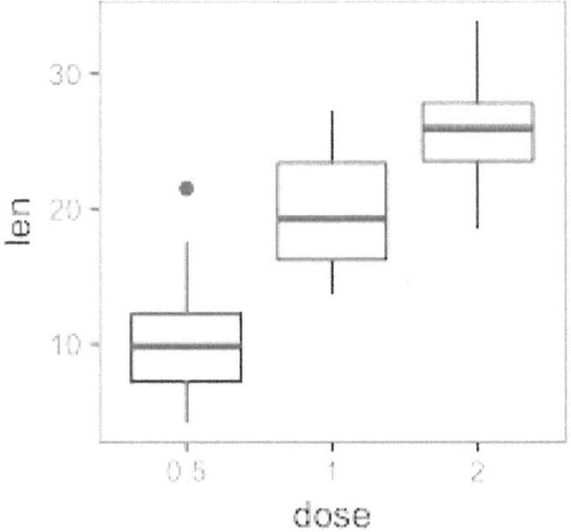

Figure 30: Grouped Box Plot

Uses of Box Plots:

- **Data Distribution Analysis:**
  - ○   Summarizing the spread and central tendency of data.
- **Outlier Detection:**
  - ○   Identifying unusually high or low values outside the whiskers.
- **Comparison of Groups:**
  - ○   Comparing variability, medians, and ranges across categories.
- **Understanding Skewness:**
  - ○   Visualizing whether data is symmetrical or skewed.
- **Highlighting Variability:**
  - ○   Showing differences in spread among datasets.

CONCLUSION

Charts play an indispensable role in analytics by fostering a clear understanding of data, driving actionable insights, and enabling effective communication. In a world where data-driven decisions are crucial, the ability to use and interpret charts effectively is a cornerstone of analytical success.

POINTS TO BE REMEMBERED

Data summarization simplifies large datasets into meaningful statistics, such as mean, median, and range. Charts, like bar charts, line graphs, pie charts, scatter plots, heat maps, and box plots, visually represent data, revealing patterns, trends, and relationships. These tools help in quick analysis, comparison, and effective communication of insights.

KEY WORDS

Summary Statistics
Centrality
Mean
Median
Range
Standard Deviation
Visualization
Charts
Bar Chart
Line Chart
Pie Chart
Scatterplot
Heatmaps
Boxplot

MULTIPLE CHOICE QUESTIONS

1. What is the primary purpose of data visualization?
    a.   Storing data
    b.   Displaying raw data for manual analysis
    c.   Communicating insights from data effectively
    d.   Organizing data into rows and columns

2. What is data summarization?

    a. Storing raw data in databases
    b. Analyzing trends over time
    c. Condensing large datasets into key statistics or insights
    d. Visualizing data using graphs

3. Which of the following is a common measure of central tendency?

    a. Mean
    b. Variance
    c. Range
    d. Standard deviation

4. What does the median represent in a dataset?

    a. The most frequently occurring value
    b. The arithmetic average of all values
    c. The middle value when data is ordered
    d. The difference between the maximum and minimum values

5. What is the range of a dataset?

    a. The average of all data points
    b. The spread of data from the smallest to largest value
    c. The middle value in ordered data
    d. The frequency of the most common value

6. Which measure identifies the most frequently occurring value in a dataset?

    a. Median
    b. Mode
    c. Mean
    d. Range

7. If a dataset is symmetric, what can be said about its mean and median?

    a. Mean is greater than the median
    b. Median is greater than the mean
    c. Mean and median are approximately equal
    d. No relationship between the mean and median

8. Which of the following is NOT a common chart type in data visualization?

   a. Bar chart
   b. Line chart
   c. Pie chart
   d. Text table

9. What does a line chart primarily represent?

   a. Categories
   b. Trends over time
   c. Proportions
   d. Hierarchies

10. Which chart type is best suited for showing proportions or percentages of a whole?

    a. a) Scatter plot
    b. b) Pie chart
    c. c) Line chart
    d. d) Histogram

11. What is the key purpose of a scatter plot?

    a. Showing relationships between two variables
    b. Comparing categorical data
    c. Visualizing time-based trends
    d. Displaying the distribution of a single variable

12. In a bar chart, what does the height of each bar represent?

    a. The trend of the variable
    b. The frequency or value of the category
    c. The correlation between variables
    d. The proportion of a whole

13. What is the term for using color gradients in visualizations to represent data intensity?

    a.   Gradient mapping
    b.   Color coding
    c.   Conditional formatting
    d.   Heatmapping

14. Which axis typically represents the independent variable in a chart?

    a.   X-axis
    b.   Y-axis
    c.   Z-axis
    d.   Both X and Y

15. Which of the following is NOT a best practice in data visualization?

    a.   Keeping the design simple and uncluttered
    b.   Using appropriate chart types for the data
    c.   Overloading the chart with excessive details
    d.   Labeling axes and data clearly

ANSWERS:

1. c. 2. c. 3. a. 4. c. 5. b. 6. b. 7. c. 8. d. 9. b. 10. b. 11. a. 12. b. 13. d. 14. a. 15. c.

CONTENT QUESTIONS FOR DISCUSSION

1.   What is data summarization, and why is it important?
2.   How does the mean, median, and mode differ in summarizing data?
3.   What role do charts play in data summarization?
4.   Explain the purpose of a box plot in data analysis.
5.   When would you use a scatter plot instead of a bar chart?
6.   How does a pie chart help in visualizing data proportions?
7.   What is the significance of identifying outliers in a dataset?
8.   Describe how a heat map can be used for data visualization.
9.   How can summarizing data support decision-making processes?
10. Why is data visualization crucial for interpreting summarized data?

EPILOGUE

The chapter discussed the process of data summarization which involves condensing large datasets into key statistics, like mean, median, and range, to identify trends and patterns. Further, the concept of data visualization using charts and graphs, such as bar charts, line graphs, and pie charts, to visually represent this summarized data, making it easier to interpret, analyze, and communicate insights was covered.

CONNECT TO THE NEXT

Having got introduced to the steps related to data summarization and visualization, the next chapter discusses about data bases, data warehousing and data mining.

REFERENCES

https://www.taxmann.com/post/blog/practical-insights-on-data-summarization-and-visualization-strategies

https://fri-datascience.github.io/course_ids/handbook/summarizing-data-basics.html

https://corporatefinanceinstitute.com/resources/data-science/kurtosis/

CHAPTER 04

Databases, Data Warehousing and Data Mining

Tagline – "Effective Data Management"

PROLOGUE

The process of collecting, organizing and storing an organization's data towards data driven decision making is a significant aspect. This is due to the fact that organizations have generated huge volumes of data. Understanding the data, organizing them and storing them in a cost-effective manner is significant from a business perspective. Hence, solutions which involve making sense of the vast quantities of data have become popular.

CHAPTER OUTLINE

A. TYPES OF DATA SOURCES
B. RELATIONAL DATABASE VS NON-RELATIONAL DATABASE
C. STRUCTURED VS UNSTRUCTURED DATA
D. DATA WAREHOUSE VS DATABASES
E. COLUMNAR DATA STRUCTURE
F. DATA MINING
G. ASSOCIATION RULES AND CLUSTERING

LEARNING OBJECTIVES

Data warehouse is a significant resource in order to convert all the data businesses generate into meaningful insights. It plays a significant role in the data management process by making it seamless and effective to analyze large volumes of information.

A. TYPES OF DATA SOURCES

Data Collection is the process of gathering, extracting, collecting, and storage of data. The data gathered used for analytics is usually voluminous. Data can exist in various forms of structured or unstructured which are nothing but audio, video, text, and image files. The step of data collection is the first step in data analysis. The data should be collected from various relevant valid sources, patterns are identified to derive insights using descriptive analytics and further predictive analytics is conducted.

Data sources can be classified based on the purpose of usage of data.

- Statistical Data - Statistical data is the data that is collected for official purposes like any surveys conducted
- Non-Statistical Data - Non-Statistical data is the data that is gathered and used for administrative purposes

Sources of data can also be classified based on its collection methods, which are –

- Internal Sources of Data - Internal sources of data are the data that is gathered within the organization itself. Example: An organisation is trying to find out the best performers in a project.
- External Sources of Data - Data may also be collected from various sources outside the organization for analytical purposes. Such sources of data collection are known as external sources of data. Example: As a patient, one can analyse the price charts of nearby hospitals for the treatment of ulcer.

B. RELATIONAL DATABASE VS NON-RELATIONAL DATABASE

A database is a collection of data that is organized in a specific manner. A database can be either a relational database or a non-relational database. A relational database is a database that stores data in tables that are related to each other. A non-relational database is a database that does not store data in tables. A relational database is a type of database that stores data in tables. Each table stores information about a specific topic, and the tables are linked together by common fields. This type of database is easy to use and understand, making it a good choice for small businesses and individual users.

B.1. SQL databases (Relational)

SQL is the short form for Structured Query Language, basically meaning a very firm way of sorting through data in the form of tables, columns, and rows. How is data structured in an SQL database? The table itself would be made up of one variable or object that we would be looking through. The column would represent the data point itself that needs to be stored and the row is a record of the data points per column. All queries posed to the database would be related to a particular table and the structure of the table would allow for easy sorting, filtering, computations, etc.

If we ever need to establish a connection between tables, say, one wants to know the weather conditions at a certain time and relate that to a baseball game's predicted score, then we need to create a key. This key enables the connection between two or more tables to solidify associations among them.

B.2. NoSQL (non-relational) databases

A non-relational database is a type of database that does not store data in tables. Instead, this type of database uses a hierarchical structure to store data. Non-relational databases are often used by large businesses and organizations that need to manage complex data. A NoSQL database is one that is less structured/confined in format, and thus, allows for more flexibility and adaptability. If one is dealing with a dataset that is not clearly defined, meaning not organized or structured, we will not have the luxury of establishing defined tables and relationships amongst the datasets.

Facebook Messenger uses a NoSQL database, because the information that is being gathered is not structured enough to be segmented into tables and define relationships between each other. With tons of unstructured information, it needs to be held in a non-relational database. Think of the information as being stored on one large word document. As more information gets entered, the document gets lengthier. If one wants to find and pull-out data, in essence 'control/command + F' can be used for the search.

Some of the popular NoSQL databases include:

- Mongo DB
- Google cloud Fire store
- Cassandra
- Apache HBase
- Amazon DynamoDB

Pros of a Relational Database

- Data is easily structured into categories.
- Data consistency in input, meaning, and easy to navigate.
- Relationships can be easily defined between data points.

Pros of a Non-Relational Database

- Data is not confined to a structured group.
- You can perform functions that allow for greater flexibility.
- Your data and analysis can be more dynamic and allow for more variant inputs.

Criteria	Relational Database	Non-relational Database
Definition	The data is stored in tables.	It uses hierarchical structure to store data
Stored Items	The stored items have relationships with each other	The stored items can be structured, unstructured or semi-structured data.
Data Integration	Due to constraints and relationships, data integrity is high	Data integration is difficult

Storage Capacity	It is suitable for medium to large data size	Large amount of data size
Reliability	It is highly reliable database	Its reliability is low
Scalability	The scalability cost is very high	It is highly scalable
Pros	i) data integrity, ii) data accuracy, iii) normalization, iv) basic structure is easy to understand v) easy access of data due to its simplicity, vi) more secure vii) it can be multi-user	i) Can easily handle unstructured data, ii) high performance, iii) dynamic changes do not affect other items of database, iv) it is open source v) flexible data model
Cons	i) Data processing is slow, ii) there is no support for complex data types iii) expensive hardware needed for its scalability.	i) Its functionality is limited, ii) manual query language, iii) data consistency is poor, iv) backup and consistency issues
Examples	Relational database examples include MySQL, SQL Server, Oracle Database	Non-relational database examples are MongoDB, Cassandra, Document DB etc.

C. STRUCTURED AND UNSTRUCTURED DATA

C.1 Structured data

Structured data is available in almost every industry. Common examples of structured data include inventory systems, invoicing systems, product databases, data from CRM systems. Structured data can be managed using relational databases and, in this case, is stored in a tabular form. The fields contain data in a predefined format, some fields may follow a rigid format like in address or phone numbers specifying a fixed length.

Advantages of Structured Data

i.   Ease of usage for business users: Structured data is used by all types of users from entry level to business. The end users using basic spreadsheets or power users like familiarity with PL/SQL, BI

ii. Support of multiple tools: Analytical tools, relational databases and other tools like big data support structured data.

iii. Directly usable: Can be used without processing like how an employee data can be used in structured format.

Disadvantages of Structured Data

i.   Inflexible: In most cases it is difficult to make changes in the structure of structured data over time as it has a predefined structure. Data is used for the purpose for which it is designed. The user has to create the schema definition in advance and that will restrict the use cases.

ii. Complex data structure: When an organization grows in size, the data stored also increases, which results in more databases, tables, files and fields. This makes it difficult to manage structured data. There may be redundant data, overlapping between data sets and result will be low quality data.

iii. Needs data preparation: Structured data needs to be cleansed and standardised before its usage in data store.

iv. Large overhead: Data warehouses are used to store the structured data in many organizations. In order to maintain structured data huge investment is needed with additional resources.

C.2. Unstructured data

Unstructured data includes multi-media content like audio, video files, social media posts and emails. These data can be difficult to standardize and categorize. It is often a data collection than a simple single data element.

For example, a document containing text or an audio file with a collection of many topics. It cannot be considered a single element. Tools used for parsing a structured data cannot parse unstructured data for categorising the data. Unstructured data has data items stored in the form of objects and if it is kept in original state, it is referred to as schema. Users manipulate using tools or other methods whenever required.

Advantages of Unstructured data

i. Flexible: Unstructured data provides for wider variety of data including text, audio, video and source code which can be used in multiple applications.
ii. Low Overhead: Unstructured data can use scalable data lakes so processing and storage will be at a lower cost.
iii. No pre-processing: Unstructured data can be stored in its native format without any pre-processing.

Disadvantages of Unstructured data

i. Requires advanced tools: Processing unstructured data needs expertise and specialised tools.
ii. Requires advanced analytics: Users need to have understanding and skills of advanced algorithms and data science in order to understand the patterns and extract insights from unstructured data. End users without advanced analytics skills cannot work with or analyse unstructured data.
iii. Lacks visibility: In a data lake it is difficult to interpret if the data within will be useful. At times the data lakes are converted to data swamps which is not useful for the organisation. In spite of not being useful it will add cost to the organization too.

Difference Between Structured and Unstructured Data:

i. **Data model:** Structured data gives details of relationship between various data elements in the database. It makes use of a relational data model. Unstructured data has a hidden structure and does not have a set data model.

ii. **Data Storage:** Structured data is stored in relational databases in organizations. In conditions where there are large volumes of data to be processed, that is if the data is gathered from different databases, data warehouse is used. Data warehouses help centralize the data storage. Organizations store unstructured data in raw formats, not in databases. Data lakes can store large amounts of unstructured data.

iii. **Data Format:** Structured data is in the form of text, numbers and are usually presented in readable standardised format The data format is predetermined. Unstructured data does not have any predetermined data format. It comes in various forms. Examples include Video (i.e., MPW), audio include WAV, mp3.

iv. **Database Type:** Structured data resides in relational databases. The databases are stored in form of tables. The tables are intersection of rows and columns. Relational databases use SQL. Unstructured data reside in non-relational database i.e. No SQL database.

v. Structured data typically resides in a relational database, arranged in tables with rows and columns. Labels specify the data types. The schema consists of the data column and type configuration. Relational databases process data using SQL. Unstructured data uses non-relational (No SQL) database. Non-relational database uses multi data models. The non-relational database processes large volume of data and is able to handle heavy loads and processes queries faster. This type of database does not use tabular schema but usually contains collection of documents.

vi. **Ease of Use and Search:** Structured data has been there since long and has many analytical tools available and is usually easier to search and use. Unstructured data involves more complex search and analysis.

vii. **Quantitative vs. Qualitative:** Unstructured data has information that is more subjective in nature and the traditional methods cannot handle. The data is qualitative in nature. It makes use of advanced analytics tools.

D. DATABASE VS DATA WAREHOUSE

A database as discussed earlier is an organised collection of information stored such that it can be easily retrieved, maintained, accessed, and updated. The data is arranged in a table format in a database. Using data indexing it gets easier to retrieve the data needed. Let us take an example of a library which has a collection of different books in different courses. The library can be considered as a database and the book in the library is the data. The databases are managed by DBMS (data base management system).

A Data Warehouse is a platform that stores a vast amount of operational data which is gathered from multiple sources The operational data is obtained from documents used for everyday operations in the organization. It is analysed and connected in data warehouse which is not just a store house of data, but also has the configuration and tools to collect the queries and analyse the information gathered. The main idea to use data warehousing is that data stored for business can accessed by separating it from data which is in the operational system and to execute complex analytical queries handling large datasets.

D.1. Characteristic Features of a Data Warehouse:

1. **Subject Oriented:** Data Warehouse is subject oriented. The focus here is on overall business subjects, rather than considering ongoing operations. In other words, it supports the various business needs of specific users in each department. A data warehouse typically provides information on a topic (such as a sales inventory or supply chain) rather than company operations. A data warehouse is always subject oriented as it delivers information about a theme instead of organization's current operations. It can be built on a specific theme. A data warehousing process is proposed to handle information on a specific theme which is more defined rather focussing on organisations current operations.

2. **Integrated database:** A data warehouse is an integration of data gathered from multiple data sources. The data gathered is consolidated in the warehouse. There are a limited number of methods for issues such as naming conventions, conflicts, units of measure, and inconsistent values.

3. **Non-Volatile:** Data stored in the data warehouse cannot be changed or modified. Read only mode is enabled so you can.
4. **Time Variant:** A data warehouse is a time-varying database that supports organizational management that analyses business data and compares it against various time periods, such as yearly, quarterly, or specific dates.

There are structured time limits between large data sets that are maintained for all online transaction processes.

Organisations presently store and process diverse set of big data and the data used by using the data warehouse and database platforms. Databases store transactional data efficiently and make to available to various systems and users as and when required. Data warehouses gather data from various sources, aggregate data from databases and other sources. They create a unified repository that can serve as the basis for analytics, querying and reporting purpose.

D.2. Databases: How it Works

A database is a collection of data stored following a set of consistent rules. A DBMS (Database management system) is used to manage this data. DBMS provides for users to interact with this data and its various constraints using an associated query language, The most commonly used query language is Structured Query Language (SQL).

Database architecture:

Relational databases have the records arranged in the form of tables with predefined rows and columns. Rules can be set for relationship between tables, data types, and formats of contained values. Data in databases are stored and retrieved in the form of records. Every row in the database represents an event for example a transaction for a vendor. The databases are suitable for storing transactional data where records can be read, inserted, updated, and deleted. There is a lot of talk about non-relational databases. Non-relational databases are referred as NoSQL databases. These databases are best choice for storing large volume of unstructured data.

Databases are used in various departments in an organisation. The databases can be deployed on premise or on cloud or both. Databases store and process transactions for administration, logistics, operations, and various management systems. Banks use databases to manage their customers, store transaction details, product details. Travel agencies use databases and provide for flight reservation system.

Databases are mainly associated with transactional systems which deals with managing various transactions used in an organisation. The systems optimized for dealing with these transactions are referred as OLTP (online transaction processing) system. Focus is on accuracy, and efficient management of data.

D.3. Data warehouses: how it works

Data warehouse is a central, integrated repository, which contains both the past and present data. The data is gathered from various disparate internal and external sources. The data is aggregated into a system as a complete storehouse for the organisation's transactional and informational data. Data Warehouse is able to handle more complex queries than individual data stores and sources. The queries are efficiently resolved by OLAP (online analytical processing) in data warehouse.

Architecture: Data warehouse

The architecture of data warehouse has three layers.

- ➤ Client layer,
- ➤ Compute layer and
- ➤ Storage layer

The client layer consists of tools that allow users to interact with and retrieve the data from the data warehouse. It may include QRA (querying, reporting and analysis) tools and business intelligence tools. The storage layer holds the data gathered and loaded into the data warehouse using an ETL tool. The compute layer executes data processing tasks required for queries.

ETL (Extract, Transform and Load) is where analytics is applied. Data is extracted from various sources and are converted into a standardised, useful format, and loaded into a warehouse. The process is called ETL.

ELT the raw data is extracted and loaded into the data warehouse by the data engineers, data scientists. The business users can transform and standardise as and when the data is required. Data integration using ELT or ETL connects the databases to the data marts and data warehouses to provide accurate and timely insights forming the basis for business intelligence.

1.11 HDFC USING DATAWAREHOUSE

During JUNE 2003, a news was published in Microsoft website that HDFC Bank partnered with Microsoft as part of its digital transformation journey. HDFC Bank, is India's largest private sector bank. The partnership with Microsoft was that time a digital transformation journey for future and getting a business value by transforming the application portfolio, securing the enterprise with Microsoft cloud and bring a transformation in the data management techniques. HDFC Bank created a data warehouse using Microsoft's SQL SERVER 2000 and Windows 2000 Advanced Server with i-Flex's Reveleus (largest known SQL server-based data warehouse in India). The introduction of Data warehouse was an initiative for introducing Business intelligence.

Microsoft Azure was used to integrate and consolidate the enterprise database. There was consolidation of a Federated Data Lake resulting in scaling of information management capabilities resulting in enhanced enterprise reporting, and advanced analytics using artificial intelligence. Built on Microsoft Azure stack, the solution will enable the bank to democratize and monetize its data landscape catering to several business units, spanning multiple systems, reports, and processes. The solution was powered by its unified architecture, collaborative engineering environment, industry-leading security and ecosystem of AI/ML based deep learning capabilities.

In addition, the Bank will also leverage Microsoft Power Platform's industry-leading low code, no code capabilities to set up an App Innovation and

Automation Factory. The App Factory will enable the Bank to migrate, modernize and transform its application portfolio.

HDFC life used an enterprise data warehouse to manage sales, operations, and financial reporting. They felt ETL will be a primary process for preparing data models and providing timely reports. They were facing performance issues with ETL processes with on premise model. ETL processes initiated at mid night would take 12 hours to complete. Employees did not get daily reports on time, and they had to start working with previous days data almost mid-day. Slow processing, suboptimal performance resulted in declined user satisfaction. In 2021, the financial close (a process where accounting and finance teams review and reduce account balances before the accounting cycle closes) almost failed. This resulted in migration from on premise model to cloud solution, which brought about high performance, scalability, reliability, meeting deadlines and user expectations.

There was a 48% improvement across all ETL job loads, allowing business users to perform faster queries on the data warehouse. The speed for overnight processing jobs went up by 40%, and data analysts could take decisions with agility. The cloud infrastructure enhanced the processing speed and ETL job were shortened by 6 hours. The analysts got an access to critical data at the very start of the day. This improved business efficiency.

D.4. Comparison - Database, Data Warehouse, Data Mart

The databases usually store day-to-day operational data. The data warehouse is an environment set up for aggregating and analysing data. The production systems draw a direct connect to the databases and the data warehouses are usually used as internal tools for managers and stakeholders. A data warehouse is a data management system that provides a platform to support analytics and business intelligence initiatives for an entire organization. Data warehouses contain large amount of past (historical/legacy) data, transactional data, application log files. The data gathered from various sources includes structured and unstructured data. The purpose of data within a warehouse is clearly defined.

A data mart is a simple form of data warehouse which focusses on a single subject, a department or subject area. It provides quicker access to data which is required by a specific team or a department within an organization. For example, if marketing department of an organisation is looking for some data to help improve its advertising strategy of a product it will be expensive and time consuming to go through data scattered across multiple systems. So, data marts are created as data mart is focused on a single subject domain or a line of business, such as sales, finance, or marketing it would provide for quick retrieval of required data.

Organisations maintain data lakes. Data lakes store structured and unstructured data, and this is used for machine learning, data science and real-time analytics use cases. The major difference between a data warehouse and a data lake is data lakes store large amount of raw data and don't have a predefined structure and they need not know in advance how data will be used.

E. COLUMNAR DATABASE

Generally, in relational databases or tables, data is stored row wise. But when there is a large quantity of data this arrangement becomes a bottleneck. To resolve this bottleneck columnar databases were introduced.

Traditional Databases store data as a sequence in a row-wise manner. For example, if one were to keep a track of all the students in a class, then records would be in the order of a row - roll no 1, name, class are captured. This is followed by all the information about roll no 2 in a new row. In this way, similar data are not next to each other, the time to access information from drives increases with passage of time.

In a Columnar Database, the names of every employee are in a series or next to one another. All names in the "Name" column and names of the class in the "Class" columns are stored one after the other. This simplifies the process of extracting similar information as the entire columns data is grouped and stored together in a go.

The objective of designing a columnar database is to improve efficiency and scale up the speed of operations during an analytics workflow. This reduces the data storage costs and speeds up the database query performance. The query performance is improved by reducing I/O operations while executing the query. The same feature has been used in Amazon Redshift and Snowflake.

The columns are divided into groups in a Columnar Database, known as Column Families. Every Column Family has a set of logically connected columns that are generally accessed or updated together. Data other than that belonging to the column family can be stored in different Column Families and accessed separately. In a Column Family, it is not necessary that every row needs to have a value for each column and here new columns can be added dynamically.

For example, suppose a city is being surveyed, and it generates data with different categories such as the name of the person, address, gender, etc. In that case, these Databases store each Column Family separately while keeping all of the data for one category related to the same key. An application just has to read a single Column Family without reading through all of the data for an entity.

A Column-Family data store in its most basic form resembles a Relational Database. The Column-Family databases use a denormalized approach to structuring sparse data. Using compression process, the performance of analytical queries can improve dramatically. Row -oriented storage is optimal for OLTP performance, where transactions frequently for reading, writing, and updating occur every millisecond. The column-oriented approach is best suited OLAP systems for analytics.

E.1. Advantages of Columnar Database

- Useful for giving queries that involve only a few columns.
- Aggregation queries against vast amounts of data.
- Compression will be done column-wise.

E.2. Disadvantages of Columnar Database

- Data loading is incremental. So, there will be maintenance issues.
- Usage of Online Transaction Processing (OLTP)
- Queries will be applied using only a few rows.

The benefits of using a Columnar Database are as follows:

Higher speed and efficiency: Columnar databases process the analytical queries faster than other database methodologies. When JOIN operation is used to combine data from two tables in a relational database, they process it A columnar database has ability to join any number of data sets and they aggregate the results of a query into a single output.

- Compressible data: In Columnar Database, data can be highly compressed using operations such as Sum, Count, Min, Max, and Avg.
- Provides for Self-indexing: Columnar database uses less storage space than an RDBMS with the same data.
- Multiuse: In many big data applications, real time analytics, OLAP cubes columnar databases are being used. They are best for these tasks as they are excellent in loading new data quickly.

F. DATA MINING

Data mining is the process of extracting useful information from a large set of data, usually from a data warehouse or collection of linked data sets. Mining tools use statistical, mathematical, and analytics to sift through large sets of data. Data Mining is also known as knowledge discovery in data (KDD), Using data mining data is converted to useful information and from the information patterns are generated. This results in identify trends, relationships between data items to help in informed decision-making and planning.

1.12. INDIAN GOVERNMENT USES DATA MINING

(https://www.india.gov.in/spotlight/pm-gati-shakti-national-master-plan-multi-modal-connectivity)

Government needs data with analytics for taking important business decisions across various industries for the country's infrastructure development. The usage of relevant data obtained will help Government to enhance the various Governance procedures, provide for faster programme implementation, and ensure that the deliverables promised are provided in a timely and efficient manner. This would work as a great advantage to the Government.

In the area of infrastructure planning, development and decision making most crucial is how data is managed for efficiency in decisions. Indian Government thinks all the Governments policy making will be improved with data, but the project needs to start with data-driven planning.

For DST (Department of Science and Technology) which is under Ministry of Science and Technology the maps in paper format served as the main information source for decision-making, these maps were rarely updated in real-time which affected the decision-making process. Developing good infrastructure projects and measuring accurately the impact of these projects in different areas were hampered due to by

A. *Lack of database with scientific management and*
B. *Lack of infrastructure information analysis*

The data which was gathered too was mainly for a specific study or an objective, so its accuracy and dependability was questionable. The data was spread across in various locations in different organisations. and did not allow for any form of trend analysis and easy accessibility of data. Due to this reason managing and analysing infrastructure projects across the country is difficult.

The Prime Minister's plan for multi modal connectivity (Gati Shakti National Master Plan) will address problems applying data mining. Usage of data mining technology made it possible for decision-makers to use spatial d data and information, which will help in implanting the strategy effectively. The data mining plan proposed use of GIS-enabled (geographically enabled information system) mapping of infrastructure development.

Data Mining has helped Indian government to initiate a platform (Project Insight) to track tax evaders. Predictive analytics would enable authorities to predict the future of defaults and risks. Using data mining Government was able to detect frauds. Like it gathered information of more than 50,000 such users who seem existed in spite of being deregistered. Governments efforts on stopping the black money menace aided with data mining had names of more than 2.24 lakh companies been struck off from the records and over 3 lakh directors were removed from directorship as they had association with these firms. Government uses data mining to provide informed policy making.

F.1. Need for data mining:

There is a dearth of data available and collected from various sources like sensors, social media, Web logs. Data Mining provides tools to exploit these data to its fullest. It has potential to identify patterns and relationships in large volumes of data from multiple sources.

The data mining process can detect some unknown, unexpected relationships and patterns in what seems like unrelated pieces of information. Information being scattered, it has historically been difficult to analyse as complete package. Many times, there is a relationship between external factors too like demographic or economic factors that have an impact on the company's sales or performance. Most of the time the executives regularly look at sales figure's region wise, product line wise, territory wise they miss out the external factors in analysis this information. The analysis focusses on what happened but does not uncover why it happened this way and this is where data mining comes in picture and fills the gap.

Data mining considers the external factors and is able to draw correlations with external factors. In all areas external factors may not be a cause for a result but, these patterns are good indicators to guide channel. product and other related decisions. The analysis of this kind can be applied for product design to delivery and in service industry too.

F.2. History

People have been gathering, processing and analysing data from several years and the process has remained the same in multiple ways: identify the data sources, combine the data, convert to information required, use the tools suitable to analyse the data, and using the insights in an effective manner.

With advancement in database systems, hardware, and other computing systems there has been growth and advancement in tools for managing and analysing data. The changes were seen in the 1960s with the development of RDBMS (relational database management systems) technology and natural language query tools like Structured Query Language (SQL). There was no need for coded programs for managing data. This was a breakthrough for business users to explore data and dig out meaningful patterns, sequences hidden in the data.

Data Mining helps the data to interact with the users. Ask a question, get an answer, and then based on what you have learn ask another question and explore in depth the data gathered. This is the kind of exploration we can do with data mining.

Data mining is an important aspect of business intelligence. Data mining tools have provision for getting insights from big data. This includes data from sensors, IOT, social media, audio, video files.

F.3. Data mining: working

Data Mining has many methodologies but there are some data preparation steps followed in all organisations. The steps are as follows:

1. **Business Understanding:** Understand the company's present situation, the objectives for which the data mining project was initiated. There needs to be a clear definition of the project objectives, which includes identification of the problems faced, understanding the goals of the project and considering the KPIs that would be used for measuring the success.

2. **Problem Understanding and data gathering:** After a clear understanding of problem there is focus on gathering the data required. Both internal and external data are part of this exploration. Data is gathered from the internal systems and databases or as a whole from the data warehouse.

3. **Data preparation and understanding:** This step involves preparing data for analysis. It involves data cleansing to remove any inconsistencies and errors, transforming data to standardised format suitable for analysis. Data preparation is a very important step as this will transform the data for data modelling.

4. **Modelling, Evaluation, deployment:** Data modelling involves developing a model that can accurately predict outcomes on new data. Evaluation is a process where the performance of the model is evaluated using statistical measures. The assessment gives an idea how well the model will predict the outcome accurately. In the deployment step the model is deployed in the production environment

5. **User training:** The data mining team is trained to use the tools.

F.4. Data mining techniques

Data mining techniques are categorized as direct data mining and undirected data mining. Data mining techniques which can try to explain or categorize a target value (e.g. income) are direct data mining. Some of the techniques used are classification, and estimation. Undirected Data Mining are the ones where we find patterns in the data without having any guidance of a target variable. In other words, it tries to find patterns or similarities without targeting a specific value as a discovery process. Techniques used are clustering, and affinity groupings.

G. ASSOCIATION RULES AND CLUSTERING

G.1. Association

Association is a data mining technique which discovers the probability of the co-occurrence of items in a collection of items. Association Rules are the relationships given between co-occurring items. The objective of association is linking two unrelated events.

USE CASE

Data mining used in research, healthcare, education, transportation, insurance, and many other sectors. Let us take few examples.

- Service Industries: In service industries, customer feedback is very important Data mining is used to understand the customers in a better manner and bring improvements in the services, products.
- Product Development: Data Mining helps companies that manufacture, design and distributes product by analysing customer purchase patterns and predict the trends. For trend analysis it uses demographic, economic and other data.
- Manufacturing: Data Mining helps manufacturers can track production, identify production concerns, maintenance data, quality trends, repair data, production rates, and product performance data from the field to identify. Helps improve on quality, product performance.

1.13 DREsSMART USES ASSOCIATION DATA MINING

Ref: https://www.ministry.nz/architecture/dress-smart-retail-outlet-stage-7

DresSMart is an online retail store for clothes and apparel. They have different products, brands, and styles. They gathered the data and applied association mining and tried to study various customer segments. They took a sample of formal shirts and explored. They found that though there were fewer records of transactions with both ties and shirts but found that once the customers buy formal shirts there is five times chances that he buys a tie too.

DresSmart had given an option to its customers to return the undamaged product back within 30 days with full refund. Using association, they found that most of the customers who are buying ties along with shirts, the product return rates of the ties for these transactions are also 3 times more than the other return rates. This gave an indication to DresSmart that customers were finding it difficult to choose matching ties while placing the orders online along with shirts. It clearly made DresSmart understand that they had to improve this procedure on the company's website. The objective is to reduce product return rate at the same time study cross selling opportunities for ties with shirts.

Data mining helps in deriving trends, patterns, sequences, and other type of useful information from a huge volume of data. By using association rules mining, we can find interesting relationship between data items in a large-scale transaction. Using data mining we can identify strong rules between related items by using different measures.

The data mining process that involves in discovering the rules which govern associations and causal objects between set of entities is known as Association Rule Mining. It helps in discovering relationships between databases that seem to be unrelated and by applying data mining we can understand the connections between datasets.

Association rule mining is a method which is meant to find frequent patterns, correlations, associations, or causal structures from data sets that are present in various kinds of databases such as relational databases, transactional databases, and other forms of data repositories. In a set of transactions, association rule mining aims to find the rules which help us to predict the occurrence of a specific item based on the occurrences of the other items in the transaction.

Majority of machine learning algorithms work with numerical datasets, and they are mathematical in nature. But Association Rule Mining is useful for non-numeric, categorical data and uses techniques like simple counting.

An association rule uses IF THEN rules. It consists of two parts:

- an antecedent (if) and
- a consequent (then)

An antecedent is something found in data, and a consequent is something located in conjunction with the antecedent.

Let us consider some examples of the following association rule:

Example 1: "If a customer buys peanut butter, he will buy jelly."

Peanut Butter is the antecedent in the given association rule, and jelly is the consequent.

Example 2: If customer buys milk, he will buy sugar

APPLICATIONS

Market Basket analysis: In this method we analyse the association of purchased items in a single basket or single purchase. Most of the supermarkets read the data collected using barcode scanners. The database here is called the "market basket" database. It contains records of past transactions of the customers and the data can be voluminous if he is a regular customer. Every record contains the name of all the products which every customer purchases in a transaction. Using this data, the stores will understand the customers behaviour, his choice of items, preferences. Based on this information, the retailer will decide the store layout and optimise the catalogue for various items.

A single record will have a complete list of all the items purchased by a customer in a single transaction. This will help understand which group of customers are interested in purchasing which set of items and the retail store will realign the store layout and catalogue to place them optimally next to one another. For example, If the customer buys a coat, it is possible that the customer may buy tie or belt along with the coat. So, keeping the coat and tie, and belt next to each other in the store will help customers to buy the items together and improves sales for the company.

Cross marketing: In this method they work with other businesses that complement their own business and not competitors. For example, vehicle dealerships and manufacturers have cross marketing campaigns with oil and gas companies.

Catalogue design: In this method the items selected in a business catalogue are often designed to complement each other. Buying one item will lead to buying another item so that buying one item will lead to buying another item. The items are usually related to each other.

Medical Diagnosis: Association rules are applied in medical diagnosis. They help doctors to diagnose and treat patients. Association rule mining helps to determine the likelihood of illness based on multiple symptoms. Can be used to learn the disease type based on the symptoms.

Census data: The concept of Association Rule Mining is used in managing census data. Association can help in proper planning of efficient public services and other related services.

G.2. Clustering

Clustering is a data mining technique which groups data by similarities rather than pre-defined assumptions. Clusters are formed based on similarities. Can have a cluster of similar objects another cluster with dissimilar objects.

Cluster analysis is a technique to group similar observations into a number of clusters based on the observed values of several variables for each individual. The data is divided into different groups by combining similar objects into a group. This group is called a cluster. A cluster is a set of similar data which is grouped together.

For example, consider a data set of fruits given in which it contains information about different fruits like apples, oranges pear, another example can be like data set of different vehicles like two-wheeler, three- wheeler or four-wheeler.

Clustering is used by any organisation that needs to identify discrete groups of customers, customer behaviour, vendor transactions or other types of behaviours. For example, banks use for credit score ranking, insurance providers use cluster analysis to detect fraudulent claims. Another example is group similar customer segments based on their purchasing patterns to give them offers or discounts. The basic objective of cluster analysis is to find groups of similar subjects, where "similarity" between each pair of subjects.

G.3. Types of clustering

Hierarchical Cluster Analysis

In this method a cluster is made first and it is then added to another cluster. This cluster will be

the most similar and closest one to form a single cluster. The process is repeated till all data items/subjects are in one cluster. This method is referred as Agglomerative method. Agglomerative clustering starts with single objects and starts grouping them into clusters. When clustering starts with full data set and then divides into partitions it known a divisive method. The divisive method is another kind of Hierarchical method in which clustering starts with the complete data set and then starts dividing into partitions.

Centroid-based Clustering

In this type of clustering, data is organised into non-hierarchical clusters, k-means method of clustering is used in this method, where k are the cluster centres and objects are assigned to the nearest cluster centres. The main idea of this method is to find k centroids followed by finding k sets of points which are grouped based on the proximity to the centroid such that the squared distances of the points in the cluster to the centroid are minimised.

Distribution based Clustering

In this method of clustering, we follow the method used in statistics for the modals of distribution. Objects that belong to the same distribution are put into a single cluster. Complex properties of objects are captured like dependence between attributes.

Density based Clustering

In this method clusters are defined by the areas of density which are usually higher than the remaining of the data set. Objects present in sparse areas are usually kept as separate clusters.

Application

Retail store clustering is where stores with similar characteristics are grouped to make purchasing inventory more effective. Rather than trying out multiple decisions related to each customer the retail teams can make decisions for buying and managing inventory for a cluster of stores. In healthcare, clustering can be used for ranking of hospitals, identification of patients having high risks, controlling infections in hospitals, identifying patients having similar disease.

CONCLUSION

In the current era where businesses are generating huge volumes of data through various devices, data management has become significant currently. Understanding the data, storing the same in data warehouses with a relational database structure would lead to data being mined in an effective manner towards effective data driven decision making. Some of the techniques covered are association rule mining and clustering.

POINTS TO BE REMEMBERED

Data management while understanding the types of data with various types of database structures. After data is stored in a data warehouse, data mining techniques like association and clustering in help in solving various business problems.

KEYWORDS

Data sources

Types of data

Structured vs unstructured data

Relational databases

Non-relational databases

RDBMS

Columnar data structure

Association rule mining

Apriori algorithm

Clustering

Types of clustering

MULTIPLE CHOICE QUESTIONS

1. Database in which data is arranged in form of tables

    a. Relational Database
    b. non-relational databases
    c. Hierarchical database
    d. Network database

2. The data type which has non-numerical data which does not have a structural framework is

    a. Structured Data
    b. Semi structured Data
    c. Unstructured data
    d. None of the options

3. In association the primary goal of generating association rules is

    a. Predict values of variables
    b. Discover relationship between variables
    c. Calculate distance from central point
    d. Calculate distance between different data points

4. Structured data is usually stored in the following format

    a. XML files
    b. HTML files
    c. JSON files
    d. Relational databases

5. Structured data is usually used in

    a. Reviewing customer support
    b. Sentiment analysis
    c. Inventory Levels in a store
    d. Audio content for promotions

6. An example of unstructured data

    a. Sensor data
    b. Customer review using sentiment analysis
    c. Inventory data
    d. Customer list with names and addresses

7. The following is an example of semi structured data

    a. Relational databases
    b. CSV files
    c. Emails with header and attachments
    d. Spreadsheets

8. A major disadvantage of using a decision tree is

    a. Can not be interpreted
    b. Prone to over fitting
    c. Expensive to train
    d. Can not be used for categorical data

9. The following is not part of pre-processing in data mining

    a. Data visualisation
    b. Data cleaning
    c. Data standardisation
    d. All the above

10. The main feature about decision trees in data mining is

    a. Used only for clustering
    b. Works with regression and classification
    c. Used for only correlation analysis
    d. All the above options

11. The main objective of clustering is

    a. Identify outliers in a dataset
    b. Reduce dimensionality
    c. To predict a continuous variable outcome
    d. To categorise datapoints into groups based on some similarity

12. DBSCAN in clustering stands for

    a. Density Based Spatial clustering of applications with Noise
    b. Density Based Spatial clustering of applications without Noise
    c. Distance Based Spatial clustering of applications with Noise
    d. Data Base Spatial clustering and network

13. In K means clustering K stands for

    a. Number of data points
    b. Number of iterations
    c. Number of clusters
    d. Name of the founder

14. In K-means clustering how are the clusters determined?

    a. Calculate distance between data points
    b. It is user-defined
    c. Chooses automatically with values given in an algorithm
    d. None of the above

15. The process of combining small clusters into larger ones in hierarchical clustering is called as

    a. K means Clustering
    b. Agglomerative clustering
    c. Divisive clustering
    d. All the above

Answers

1. a 2. c 3. b 4. d 5. c 6. a. 7. c. 8. b. 9. a. 10. b. 11. d. 12. a. 13. c. 14. b. 15. b.

CONTENT QUESTIONS FOR DISCUSSION

1. What is the primary difference between structured and unstructured data?
2. What is the difference between structured and unstructured data sources?
3. Give examples of internal and external data sources.
4. What is the difference between a relational database and a non-relational database?
5. What is a columnar data structure, and how does it store data?
6. Give examples of databases that use columnar data structures.
7. What is a relational data structure, and how is data organized in it?
8. How do tables, rows, and columns represent data in a relational model?
9. What is association rule mining?
10. How is clustering used in data mining?

EPILOGUE

The chapter discussed the type of data sources, data management aspects, relational and non-relational databases. Further, data storage in data warehouses and the data mining process was elaborated with specific techniques on association and clustering.

CONNECT TO THE NEXT

Having discussed data management, storage and mining process, the next chapter takes a leap towards trends in analytics which will be a game changer for businesses. Some of the topics include web commerce, machine learning, artificial intelligence among others.

REFERENCES

https://www.pluralsight.com/blog/software-development/relational-vs-non-relational-databases

https://databasetown.com/relational-vs-non-relational-database/

https://www.datamation.com/big-data/structured-vs-unstructured-data/

https://www.datatobiz.com/blog/data-warehousing-what-is-it-characteristics-more/

https://towardsdatascience.com/6-types-of-clustering-methods-an-overview-7522dba026ca

https://www.datanovia.com/en/blog/types-of-clustering-methods-overview-and-quick-start-r-code/

https://timesofindia.indiatimes.com/business/india-business/hdfc-implements-data-warehouse-on-sql-server-2000/articleshow/8214.cms

CHAPTER 05

Future Trends of Analytics

Tagline: "Conquer the future with data"

PROLOGUE

Analytics as a concept has played a significant role in changing the way businesses are run. The change is with respect to gaining competitive advantage, offering optimized solutions and improvement in the bottom line. Being a field which relies upon the changing technology, it will be a good idea to understand the trends which impact the field of analytics.

CHAPTER OUTLINE

- A. ROLE OF AI IN BUSINESS
- B. MACHINE INTELLIGENCE
- C. COMPETITIVE INTELLIGENCE
- D. TEXT MINING
- E. WEB ANALYTICS
- F. ROLE OF INTELLIGENT AGENTS
- G. M-COMMERCE
- H. LOCATION ANALYTICS
- I. SOCIAL MEDIA ANALYTICS
- J. CONTENT ANALYTICS
- K. SENTIMENT ANALYSIS
- L. ETHICAL CONSIDERATIONS

LEARNING OBJECTIVES

The objectives of this chapter are

- To understand the technologies and techniques that influence Business Analytics

- To understand how the various techniques influence social media analytics
- To appreciate the directive taken by organizations to process data using ethical and legal means

A. ROLE OF AI IN BUSINESS

AI in Business

Artificial intelligence has a range of use in businesses, including aggregation of business data, streamlining job processes. Artificial Intelligence is seen as a supporting tool rather than a replacement for humans. Presently AI is unable to manage common sense tasks but has the ability to process and analyse large volumes of data more rapidly than a human brain could. Artificial intelligence has the ability to make decisions, analyse patterns, give insights and these features make AI highly valuable throughout many industries – whether it is a complex task like monitoring plants in an industry or simply helping visitors find their way in a campus.

Some of the most common uses of AI are routing, recommendations, personalization, internet searches and personal assistants. Some of the applications are also in machine learning, cybersecurity, and customer relationship management.

Machine learning

Machine learning can extract structured information from unstructured data. Organisations gather a large volume of data from customers. A machine learning algorithm automates the process of understanding patterns in datasets for predictive analytics. For example, it can generate a model to predict a cardiac ailment, predict if a transaction is fraudulent or legitimate in a banking scenario.

Cybersecurity

Artificial intelligence helps to trace the loopholes in computer networks. By monitoring the input data patterns AI systems can recognize a cyberattack or even a cyberthreat. Once a threat is detected, it can backtrack the data to find the source and help to prevent a future threat.

Customer relationship management

Artificial intelligence is also changing customer relationship management (CRM) systems. Using AI, CRM system are transformed into a self-updating, auto-correcting system. AI uses a vast amount of data to identify patterns in customers' search behaviours. It looks to provide them with more relevant information to improve customer services, and target the right customer. The focus now is how information finds the right customer at the right time rather than expecting the user to constantly go to Google's search tab.

Digital personal assistant

Artificial intelligence is not just to create a more customised experience for the customers but can be even transforming the way a company operates from inside. AI bots can be used as personal assistants to help manage emails, maintain calendar, and even provide recommendations for streamlining processes.

1.14 LG ELECTRONICS USING AI FOR AUTOMOTIVE PARTS

LG Electronics (LG) collaborated with Altair, and jointly developed an AI validation platform that delivered enhanced reliability verification for various vehicle parts. Altair is a global provider of computational science and artificial intelligence (AI) solutions. The technology was integrated into the development process which allowed LG to provide global automakers with advanced infotainment solutions. These solutions were of the highest quality and reliability.

Earlier the process used for developing advanced vehicle components was dependent on physical testing and these all-test results had to be manually validated. LG's digitalization of testing and verification resulted in cost reduction and provided for data and product reliability.

The new platform uses machine learning algorithm and applies time series analysis, data analysis visualization, and various other functions which enhances LG's already-stringent component verification system. The AI validation platform provided for detailed reports that helped to assess the new platform with respect to the quality of yet-to-be-commercialized products with a greater degree of precision. The advanced platform is expected to secure a product reliability rate of 90 percent or higher.

LG plans to use AI technology in other processes like product planning, mass production, and other areas. According to Eun Seokhyun, president of the LG Vehicle component Solutions (VS) Company stated that their new AI verification platform is a meaningful digitalization case for the automotive parts business, where reliability is of the highest importance. He further adds that LG is committed to digital transformation of all its global operations and use of AI will help in optimal resource management.

AI in Sales

Email campaigns are effective means in sales and marketing to get results. But for a company to send multiple mails and tracking their responses can be exhausting. With AI solutions, email responses are monitored, categorised, and grouped as per requirements. The manual way of monitoring of replies and flagging the unwanted emails is removed using AI.

Demand forecasting

Forecasting is complex, but they can be automated. Artificial intelligence enables the creation of automated and accurate sales projections based on all client interactions and historical sales results.

Lead Scoring

AI tools help sales professionals prioritise customers based on their probability to convert. With AI, the algorithm can rank the leads in the pipeline.

B. MACHINE INTELLIGENCE

Machine intelligence is presently used in major industries in manufacturing and service industries. Machine intelligence is expected to be used more widely as research into technology continues to grow. Machine intelligence is the basis of machine learning and artificial intelligence as the machine learns to work proactively. If any machine learns to extract different types of data to put together its own processes and has ability to arrive at its own conclusions, we can say that that it is machine intelligence based on functionalities of machine learning and artificial intelligence.

When machines are programmed with some aspects of human intelligence, includes qualities like learning, problem solving and decision making then it is Machine intelligence. Any machine can solve a complex set of problems with limited abilities. A system depicting true machine intelligence has the ability to know when they make mistakes, so next time it sees a similar data that could probably lead to a similar mistake the next time, it will avoid it. Machine Intelligence uses deductive logic.

C. COMPETITIVE INTELLIGENCE

Competitive Intelligence (CI) is the collection and analysis of information to anticipate competitive activity. It helps to understand the past market disruptions and has the capability to interpret the current events too.

Some of the advantages of Competitive Intelligence are the ability to

- Identify and analyze industry trends to decide on future plans.
- Gather knowledge and insights into future trends, and technologies.
- Analyze strengths and weaknesses.
- Allocate resources more efficiently.
- Enhance return on investment
- Improve competitor surveillance
- Make effective business decisions.

Competitive Intelligence has scope in multiple scenarios. It can help develop corporate or business unit strategies. It is used to prepare a new product launch, new market entry, or any other strategic decisions in market. It helps organizations plan for future market opportunities and disruptions. It also helps assess the competitors' market position and product promotion strategies.

In general, Competitive Intelligence activities are applied in two ways:

- **Tactical** - a short-term process like how to capture the market, improve profits
- **Strategic** - helps with long-term processes like what opportunities a company can face

Sources to derive Competitive Intelligence

- Social media platforms: Analysis of customers' feedback on various social media platforms helps compare your products with the competitors' products/services.
- Sites of competitors: Competitors' websites help to analyze their products and services, and this gives an insight into their business.
- Syndicated research reports: Gives an overview of your market, major competitors, and identify the unique selling propositions.
- Marketing tests: Using A/B testing and other methods we can monitor the competitor's campaign and find out what works best and what doesn't need to be executed.
- Product reviews: Analyzing third-party product reviews helps to determine who are the customers of your competitors and what are their likes and dislikes about their products or services.
- Pricing and packaging updates: Changes made to packaging and pricing also affect marketing campaigns.

Competitor intelligence: How to conduct Competitor Intelligence

Identify direct and indirect competitors:

First step is to know the competitors. Identifying at least the top five direct competitors. Then determine the indirect (firms in the same industry that do not compete with the company for customers), or perceived competitors (businesses that can crop up suddenly during the sales discovery process but do not compete with you). Understanding the competitors helps to understand the competitive environment.

Choose the focus areas:

Once the competitors are identified, data collection is conducted. All the information is thus gathered online and from the front-line teams.

Gather necessary additional information:

In this step detailed information on the competitors' sites, products, social media platforms, and content is obtained.

Conduct competitive analysis:

The trends are identified and then, the information is organized in the right manner to convey it to all the teams. Competitors' profiles are created, and they continue to track various updates with regard to changes in products or services and customer reviews.

Share the findings:

To improve the strategies, the findings are shared with stakeholders. This is done by conducting a meeting, sending emails, or using an internal chat. The data is stored on a reliable platform so that the team can get an easy access to the information obtained.

A good example of competitive intelligence is how airlines price the tickets. They change the prices of their tickets every day based on the information they obtain. For instance, if competitors increase the prices on a certain route the company will do the same to receive good revenue. The airline companies track the actions of potential customers to make price adjustments. For example, they spot users who search for the same flight details several times and increase prices.

1.15 SAP USES AI

*Any company's most valuable assets are its workforce. SAP used AI for human capital management (HCM) that helped the organisation to attract, retain, and skill up their employees. In **SAP SuccessFactors Recruiting** there are new generative AI capabilities that enable hiring managers to give job descriptions with accuracy. It has the capability to capture the desired skills and attributes of each role. It also generates interview questions designed to specific job descriptions and candidates' resumes. The use of AI saves hiring manager's time.*

SAP makes use of SuccessFactors Software which has AI capabilities, and it enhances people's skills, competencies, capabilities, work style and provides them with recommendations to grow and develop. The recommendations act as a guide and provide support to their employees by giving them suggestions through mentoring programs. This even helped to gain a better understanding of skill sets in their workforce to improve internal mobility, retention, and workforce agility.

SAP uses AI in its supply chain, and this helps to predict and respond to the real time demands. SAP transportation management has AI capabilities that processes multiple delivery notes received daily in various formats and the automation prevents errors in data entry. The SAP Extended Warehouse Management, uses AI for an intelligent slotting mechanism which will suggest how to optimise stocks, warehouse organisation, and replenish stocks based on a product's demand, features or as forecasted. This will improve the efficiency in warehouse management.

In procurement, SAP uses AI to help reduce costs and increase compliance across different markets. SAP Business Network has an intelligent invoice converter that makes it easier for procurement teams to onboard new suppliers The system can automatically extract, and process required information from the supplier invoices.

In finance, SAP uses AI to automate, provide recommendations and give insights in all its finance operations. SAP S/4 HANA helps to forecast the late payment risks on an invoice and investigates customers who require regular follow up. Risk management process is simplified and there is a better mechanism to manage the capital and liquidity.

D. TEXT MINING

Text mining is a part of data mining that deals specifically with unstructured text data. It makes use of natural language processing (NLP) techniques to extract useful information and gain insights from large amounts of unstructured text data. Text mining can be used as a pre-processing step for data mining or as a standalone process for specific tasks. In other words, we can say text mining is the process of extracting essential data from standard language text. All the data we obtain from emails, text messages, documents, files are written in common language text.

SEO (Search engine optimization) is a set of strategies used to promote some content which is obtained from the search results. Google uses Text mining with visualisation techniques to find the gap between what the users search and what they get. It helps to create some content that bridges the gap, and relevant search results are shown on top.

Importance of text mining

Most of the business data consists of unstructured information such as text. Text mining helps the businesses extract more valuable information from the unstructured text generated every day through email messages, social media posts, customer service tickets, chatbots and other sources. It can be extremely time-consuming or even impossible to analyse all this information without an automated process. Automatic processing of text documents can also produce more accurate and consistent information. Text mining helps businesses to respond quickly and provide more personalised customer service.

Text mining vs Text analytics

Text analytics is a term used to describe a further analytical step after text mining. Text mining extracts qualitative information, such as customer sentiment whereas text analytics provides more quantitative statistical analysis of this information. The analysis is often presented in a visual form such as graphs, charts or tables. For example, applying text analytics to customer service emails categorised as having a negative sentiment could generate a customer churn analysis chart indicating the percentage of customers that are complaining about product price, delivery, quality or technical support.

Text mining: How does it work

Text Mining software uses NLP (natural language processing) along with ML (machine learning) and rule-based systems to discover patterns, sequences and relationships in the text documents.

Unstructured data is pre-processed using NLP and after pre-processing, data is ready for machine learning models to be applied. The models use machine learning to recognise patterns. The model is first fed with text documents manually tagged as belonging to a certain category. From the training input data set, the machine learning system creates a predictive model. The new documents are then fed to the predictive model, which assigns the appropriate classification.

Cleansing/Cleaning - Removing small words (a, an, to, the) and correcting misspellings.

After pre-processing of data some common text mining techniques are applied as follows:

Information retrieval (IR) technique is based on some pre-defined set of queries, it provides the relevant documents based on the queries. IR systems track user behaviours with appropriate algorithms. Common example where IR is used is in popular search engines like Google Information retrieval is com.

Some common Information Retrieval tasks include:

- Stemming - Reducing a word to its stem by removing prefixes and suffixes ("hear" is the stem for both "hearing" and "heard," for example). This technique improves information retrieval by reducing the size of indexing files.

- Tokenizing - Process of breaking out long-form text into sentences and words which area called as "tokens". They are used in the models, like bag-of-words, for text clustering and document matching tasks. Dividing text into distinct words and phrases.

NLP (Natural language Processing): The sentence structure and grammar is analysed. The NLP sub-tasks include:

- **Tagging:** Tagging is also known as Part of speech (PoS) tagging. Here the various parts of speech within text, such as nouns, verbs and adjectives are identified. A tag is assigned to every token in a document based on what part of speech: nouns, verbs, adjectives, etc. it is representing. This step enables semantic analysis on unstructured text.
- **Parsing syntax:** Analysing the structure of sentences and phrases to determine the role of different words. This identifies the subject, verb and object of a sentence, for example.
- **Text classification:** This task, which is also known as text categorisation. It analyses text documents and classifying them based on some categories or predefined topics. It is useful when categorising synonyms and abbreviations.
- **Summarization:** In this technique we get a summary of a document's main points.

Information extraction (IE) surfaces the relevant pieces of data when searching various documents. It also focuses on extracting structured information from free text and storing these entities, attributes, and relationship information in a database. Common information extraction sub-tasks include:

- Feature selection, or attribute selection, is the process of selecting the important features (dimensions) to contribute the most to output of a predictive analytics model.

- Feature extraction is the process of selecting a subset of features to improve the accuracy of a classification task. This is particularly important for dimensionality reduction.
- Name-entity recognition (NER) also known as entity identification or entity extraction, aims to find and categorize specific entities in text, such as names or locations. identifies "Delhi" as a location and "Diya" as a woman's name.

APPLICATIONS

1. **Health Sector:** In healthcare, patient management and engagement right from studying the patient history to various medication in various dosages, text analytics plays a role. This helps where patient notes have been used to predict treatment for certain symptoms.
2. **Insurance Sector:** Text analytics helps in managing portfolios by reducing the risks involved. This is also used in claims automation, policy review and processing.
3. **Email filtering:** Email system providers use text mining to identify distinct features of spam emails and phishing messages in emails, automatically deleting the messages before they are delivered to employees. This helps businesses minimise the risk of cyberattacks.

E. WEB ANALYTICS

"Data are just summaries of thousands of stories – tell a few of those stories to help make the data meaningful." - Chip & Dan Heath, Authors of Made to Stick. Metrics like page views can begin to tell a larger story of a visit, session or path. Web analytics plays an important role here. Several metrics like page views can begin to tell a larger story of a visit or a session. Most organisations and businesses have established their online presence. But with the huge data and traffic that online platforms offer, it might become difficult for businesses to gain a complete outlook of their online consumers' behaviour. This is where web analytics comes into the picture.

Web analytics offers data about your website, your visitors, and their behaviour so that you can analyse what is working and what is not and recover your website's performance and conversion rates. Website data analytics tools help companies to get detailed information on the demographics, user behaviour, age, gender, and source of traffic. Using web analytics, organisations can gain direct insights into how the website is acting and what the customers are saying about the products or services.

In Web analytics we gather and analyse data using web analytics tools to track what happens on the company's site and answers important questions, including:

- How many people visited your site?
- Where do they reside?
- Which pages did they visit?
- How much time they spend on the company's site?
- How many leave without viewing important pages?

These insights help you ensure your site is user-friendly.

Steps in Web Analytics

1. **Set the objectives:** The first step in the web analytics process is to determine the objectives and purpose of applying Web Analytics. The objectives include enhanced sales, improved customer satisfaction and brand awareness.
2. **Data Gathering:** The next step in web analytics is data collection and data storage. Organisations gather data directly from a website or web analytics tool, such as Google analytics. The data is gathered mainly from Website (https) requests, and it can be combined with external data. For example, a user's IP (internet protocol) is typically associated with many factors, including the location etc.
3. **Data processing:** The data gathered is processed to generate actionable information.

4. **Identifying key performance indicators (KPIs):** KPI is a quantitative measure to monitor and analyse user behaviour on a website. Examples include user sessions, bounce rates and on-site search queries.
5. **Developing a strategy:** Strategies are formulated aligning with organisation goals involves implementing insights to formulate strategies that align with an organisation's goals. For example, search queries conducted on-site can help an organisation develop a content strategy based on what users are searching for on its website.
6. **Experimenting and testing:** Businesses try different strategies and select the one that yields the best results. For example, using A/B testing can be used to find how customers respond to different content.

Types of Web Analytics

Web analytics can be categorised into two major categories:

1. Off-site web analytics
2. On-site web analytics

Off-site web analytics

Off-site web analytics refers to monitoring of visitors' activity. This is done outside of an organisation's website usually to measure the prospective audience. It provides an insight of how well the business is performing compared to their competitors. There is a focus on data gathered across the web like search engines, social media platforms and forums. Off-site analytics gives an industry wide analysis.

On-site web analytics

On-site web analytics focusses on specific site. It refers to tracking the activity of visitors on a specific site to monitor how well the site is performing. Here data gathered is usually more useful to a site's owner and can have details like which content is most frequently viewed, site engagement duration and other relevant details. The common methods used include log file analysis and page tagging.

Log file analysis is analysing data gathered from log files to monitor and report on the performance of a website. Log files contain record of every activity on the network server including web server, database server, file server.

Page tagging is adding pieces of code into a website's hypertext and markup language code to track website visitors and their interactions across the website. These pieces of code are referred as tags. When organisations add tags to a website, they can be used to track multiple metrics, such as the pages viewed, number of visitors, products viewed, number of pages viewed.

Importance of Web Analytics

Web analytics helps to track what is happening on the site and identifies areas for improvement in terms of content and user experience. It focuses on Web optimisation. It can improve ROI, increase conversions, and website traffic if performed correctly. Let us see observe few measures which would help achieve the best outcomes through Web analytics.

1. **Check the number of conversions:** Website analytics is able to achieve optimisation of conversion rate. This means increasing the percentage of visitors who become paid customers or subscribers. Once conversion rate is known we can effectively determine what website's content drives visitors to perform desired actions, whether if it is lead or sales. In it can be found where the users drop off and the company can make changes to enhance user experience and this improvement can lead to conversions.

For example, a university offering online courses wants to increase the number of users signing up for various courses. They offer a day or two free sessions for students to experience the course and then they see how many students sign up for only free sessions or how many enrol for paid courses by using web analytics to track the conversion rate and how many students drop off after the free sessions. The university can make changes based on the results by providing more details of future benefits of the course or provide better user interface and this will lead to increase its number of students enrolling for paid courses and in turn increase revenue.

2. **Understanding the audience:** It is always good to know who are the users visiting the company's site. This gives a view of different users' persona. Web analytics helps to understand more about user demographics, their behaviour and this way the web content and product offering can be designed as per user specific needs. We can also identify the channels that drive the most traffic and look into conversions to the website and how to improve their performance.

3. **Understand how audience navigate:** It is desirable to know how the users navigate the company's website, which includes what pages they visited, how often they visit, and how much time they spend on each page. This will gain an understanding of what the audience is looking for and what is of value to them. The web analytics data helps the company to design the site and provide information for the users in the company site. The content in the site can be curated as per user requirements.

4. **Identify pages driving maximum traffic:** It is good to find out what pages drive the maximum traffic on the company's website. In this way users' preferences can be understood and marketing strategies and other decisions can be planned accordingly.

Metrics of Web Analytics

Traditional web analytics help to understand who visits the company website and how they interact with its content. There are nowadays tools like Google Analytics, Mixpanel, Matomo, and Adobe Analytics to gather this data. Each of these software tracks metrics. Google Analytics (GA) is the most commonly used tool by many companies.

Some of the metric used by various tools are as follows

1. Acquisition based metrics

Acquisition based metrics measure how to get visitors to visit the website. For this, there is a need to understand who the visitors are and how did they land up in the companies' website.

These metrics include:

   a. **Users:** On a selected date/date range visitors browsed the site. This metric helps to measure the audience size and determines if the company is targeting the right audience.
   b. **New users:** On a specific date / date range how many unique users visited the site. This metric helps to determine if the site is able to attract new people visiting for the first time.
   c. **Sessions:** includes all the user interactions within a specified time framework. This metric helps to understand what user does when he visits the company website.

2. Behavior-related metrics

Behaviour related metrics measures people's behaviour when they visit the company's website. It will help to understand visitors' behaviour patterns, such as their engagement on the site, the most popular pages, activities involved by user on the site. These metrics include:

a. Bounce rate: It tracks the user's activity when he visits a website page and leaves without making another request. For example, if a user visits the websites takes no action and leaves after viewing a page this is called as bounce rate. It is determined by calculating the number of bounces over the total number of pageviews to a page. A bounce occurs whenever a user enters the page and then exits without visiting another page on the website or viewing any of the elements on the page.

b. Exit rate: Exit rate determines how often a user leaves the website from a single page. When we know which pages the visitors are exiting the most and at what percentage then improvements can be done on this page. Exit rate is determined by the number of people who exit the website after landing on a page and compares it to the total number of views the page received.

c. Pages per session: This is the average number of pages the users view on the website during a session. This helps to determine how engaged the visitors are on the website. For example, a high value of pages/session shows that visitors were very active viewing the web site found useful information on the website.

d. Session duration: This is the average time a user spends on a website in a single session. A long session indicates that visitors find the website's content relevant and engaging, while a short session may indicate that the website is not designed as per their needs or expectations.

3. Conversion-related metrics

Conversion-related metrics measure how many people after landing on the website take a desired action. This tells how many users are converted to prospective users and how much revenue the company earns.

These metrics include:

a. **Ecommerce conversion rate:** the percentage of visitors who purchase the product or take the services after visiting the site. The metric helps to find how effectively the website converts visitors into purchasing.

b. **Transactions:** the metric provides insights into the number of customer purchases, the average value of the transactions, and the total revenue the company generated from sales.

c. **Revenue:** the amount of money generated from the transactions on the companies' website. This metric tracks the return on investment for the marketing campaigns and advertising efforts taken by the company.

Web Analytics Tools

Based on how data is gathered there are two main web analytics tools

a. **On-site/hosted:** Here a small portion of code is installed on will generate analytics unique to you (e.g., Google Analytics or Clicky)

b. **Third-party/off-site:** Here insights are collected from third-party sources (like search engines and toolbars) which generates analytics data about multiple websites.

Within these categories we have different web analytics software some of the category functions may overlap. The categories are as follows:

1. **Traditional analytics tools:** Gathers quantitative website traffic data, like bounce rate and pageviews (e.g., Google Analytics)
2. **Behaviour analytics tools:** Gathers the individual user or aggregate qualitative user website behaviour data (e.g., Hotjar)
3. **Customer journey analytics tools:** Gathers the customer touchpoint data across various channels (e.g., Woori)
4. **Content analytics tools:** Gathers analytics data to measure website content performance (e.g., Chartbeat)
5. **SEO analytics tools:** Gathers data on keyword performance, backlinks, search traffic, and competitors (e.g., SEMrush)

Here are some top Web analytics tools:

1. Google Analytics
2. Monster Insights
3. Hubspot
4. Mixpanel
5. Google Optimize
6. Hotjar
7. SemRush
8. Matomo
9. Chartbeat
10. Similar

F. INTELLIGENT AGENTS

An agent is anything that uses sensors to perceive the environment and act upon that environment through actuators. An agent can be a software agent, intelligent enough to conduct activities on its own. An Intelligent agent is a program that can take decisions or perform an action based on its environment or inputs given by users. The programs can be used to autonomously gather information on a regular, designated schedule or when prompted by the user in real time. Intelligent agents are also referred to as a bot, which is short form for robot. In an intelligent agent program, the agent uses the parameters the user provides, and searches portions or the entire internet. After searching, it gathers the information the user is looking for and provides it to the user on a periodic or requested basis. Intelligent agents can extract any specific information, such as some keywords or date.

Intelligent agents learn from experience. It focuses on real time problem solving, analysis of success or failure rates and the use of memory-based storage and retrieval. Organisations can use intelligent agents for applications in data mining and data analytics and customer service support (CSS). Intelligent agents are also similar to software agents which are autonomous computer programs.

Types of intelligent agents

Based on the capabilities and level of intelligence, intelligent agents are categorised as:

1. **Reflex agents:** Agents that ignore the past and investigate the present state are known as reflex agents. The response is based on the ECA rule (event-condition-action). Here a user initiates an event and the agent looks into the list of pre-defined rules and pre-programmed results.
2. **Model-based agents:** Agents that are like reflex agents in terms of choosing an action, but they have a more comprehensive view of the environment. In the internal system containing the agent's history a model of the environment is programmed.
3. **Goal-based agents:** Agents that are like model-based agents but store information regarding goals or information about desirable situation.
4. **Utility-based agents:** Agents that are similar to goal-based agents but provide for utility measurement. Utility measurement helps to compare each scenario based on the results obtained and chooses the results that work best.
5. **Learning agents:** Agents that have the ability to improve over a period of time and become more knowledgeable about an environment by adding

more learning elements. The feedback from the learning element is taken to improve the performance over a period of time.

Examples of intelligent agents

Alexa and Siri, AI agents are examples of intelligent agents. They make use of sensors to take a request from the user and then automatically collect data from the internet without the user's intervention. They can be used to gather information about its perceived environment such as weather and time.

Infogate (gives alerts to users about news based on specified topics of interest). Autonomous vehicles (use sensors, GPS and cameras to take decisions based on the environment) are examples of intelligent agents.

Some intelligent agents mimic human thought process and behaviour and are able to make decisions on their own, learn, and interact with other intelligent agents. Intelligent agents can be stationary or mobile varieties, i.e., they either reside in a system or can be transferred from one server to another to perform various activities autonomously. A true intelligent agent must be social, adaptable, proactive and autonomous. Multi-agent intelligent agent exhibits all these features.

In an e-commerce site, intelligent agents are known as shopping bots. These shopping bots are used by consumers to see the pricing of a product or to search for a product on the web. Every shopping bot operates in a different manner, based on the business model applied. In one scenario, the shopping bot directs users to retailers who, by subscribing for a fee, are part of a closed system.

Intelligent agents provide different services to the customer on the web. They help in answering some common questions that a customer asks. They provide direct answers to some common questions. This way it will reduce the cost for the company (customer service cost). The customer will get most of his queries answered before he speaks to a customer service representative and even if he speaks the time of conversation will be reduced. Intelligent agents track customers who abandon shopping carts without purchasing any products and try to convert them from prospective to actual customers.

The market for E-commerce is large and intelligent agents can be used in the ecommerce sector to resolve some problems encountered. The common problems where intelligent agents can be useful include

- For notification: notifying of availability of a product like a new brand of shoes or author's newly launched book, notifying when the specific products are available at a specific price.
- Recommendations: retrieving information from various sources, filtering information based on contents
- Procurement: Get the materials, services into the organisation towards the end user.
- Brokerage: finding information about products, prices, vendors, sellers and prices, providing protection for privacy, validating customer's credit, and billing.

In an ecommerce scenario, it can be used in various stages of purchase process:

1. **Identification:** In this stage the buyer gets information about the product and is inspired to buy (unmet needs). Intelligent agents can play an important role to check on purchases that are repetitive or can study customer behaviour and predict the purchases. One of the common methods used is notifications or alerts.

2. **Brokering:** Product brokering and merchant brokering are two common methods used. In product brokering, once a buyer recognizes a requirement to purchase a product, he needs to determine what he wants to buy by evaluating the product information. Intelligent agents can be used to lower the consumers' search cost by reducing the time of search in deciding which products best meets their needs. The result of this is to focus on a set of goods. In merchant brokering it combines the customers› consideration from the previous stage with merchant-specific alternatives to help determine who to buy from.

3. **Negotiation:** In negotiation the price and other terms of the transaction are settled between merchants and buyers. Most of the B2B transactions involve negotiation. Negotiation costs work high for consumers or sellers. Intelligent agents can solve this problem.
4. **Payment and delivery:** This stage indicates the end of the negotiation stage or stages for placing another order. In some cases, the presented payment or delivery options can affect product and merchant brokering.
5. **Product service and evaluation:** Post purchase stage where there is evaluation of product service, customer service, and evaluation of the satisfaction levels of the customers their complete buying experience and decisions taken.

Intelligent agent for search and retrieval

There is a vast amount of data available in various databases and networks and over year it has increased and continues to increase. The search and retrieval engines available provide limits help to users in finding relevant information. Autonomous intelligent agents help in locating relevant information based on their needs. They turn the passive search and retrieval agents into active assistants. There is an index used to search the location of a document quickly.

G. M-COMMERCE

"E-commerce is exploding and mobile commerce is fastest growing segment of the e-commerce explosion." — Wireless GCN.

The mobile commerce vertical is growing at a rapid pace and the percentage share of digital purchases that are taking place on mobile devices are increasing every year. Consumers find it easier to do purchases on mobile as it is very convenient and most of the people globally have an easy access to smartphones and tablets.

We expect retail m-commerce sales to account for 43.4% of total retail e-commerce sales in 2023. They predict m-commerce sales to hit $534.18

billion, or 40.4% of ecommerce sales, in 2024. Smartphones and tablets are two main devices driving this.

1.16 APOLLO HOSPITALS USING M-COMMERCE

Indian healthcare industry's technology spending is quite low compared to other countries. Only in 2014 it crossed the $1-billion mark annually. This was the time when hospitals and clinics started to outsource IT spendings. But it was the year 2020 there was an upsurge in the spending on technology in the private healthcare sector. During this time Apollo Hospitals upgraded its Ask Apollo app to evolve into Apollo 24/7, and it was mainly done to attend to patients who could not commute as a lockdown of three months was declared. The pandemic brought a lot of changes not only in patients and their families, but also the medical staff and Apollo Hospitals' 350-member IT organisation.

Apollo 24/7, is the omni-channel online platform of Apollo Hospitals Enterprise. On 30 November 2020, more than 4600 of Apollo Hospitals' doctors completed 230,000 online consultations on the app. It has 5 million registrations, according to an investor presentation dated January 2021. The healthcare company has 71 hospitals across the country, and 10,261 beds (the largest private player in India). Apollo Hospitals also has 200 clinics, and a doctor count of 11,000, according to its 2019-20 annual report.

When the pandemic set in, Apollo had to create additional isolation centres across its physical infrastructure while attending to the existing base of patients. The first step they took was to reach out to the patients. This was done using a CRM tool and connected to the patient. The doctors, clinical staff and patients' relatives were trained to use this remote solution. Everyone was already used to handle messenger applications and chats but using it for healthcare solutions many were not familiar with. The Apollo app helped in getting more patients in addition to those who were regular visitors to the hospitals.

Apollo Hospitals' core technology team comprises 350-odd employees, but it is supported by a good set of vendors. IT services is one of the largest parts of private hospital networks' IT spends. Apollo's partner is DXC Technologies for IT application services. It has tied up with Microsoft on the entire cloud offering, Oracle for database, ERP and human capital management, Fortinet for networking gear, PwC for ERP-related IT services, and EY for security-related IT services. The core technology team has put the governance and execution layer in place for most of its 68,000 employees to be familiar with technology applications. This involved constantly working with the business and clinical teams in enhancing business practices and workflows, as technology ran the healthcare ecosystem.

When the lockdown happened if there were patients who had surgeries a few days before the lockdown, a team quickly segregated patients who needed follow up, from the patients who were on continuous healthcare programmes in specialties like oncology and neurosciences, or kidney surgery patients who needed dialysis. Preference was given to patients who were about to go into surgery. After this Apollo began to reach out to the regular care patients like those in diabetes care using the app. The app helped them to make the shift easily. They were not in an experiment but an execution stage so it was easy to make improvements, be more proactive and get a higher level of efficiency. More usage and more adoption led to more learning for improvements.

During pandemic the hospitals required isolation centres. So, the IT team created additional capacity (centres and makeshift ICU beds) like normally it would do, it would have been in a high-touch environment. But with the pandemic, it had to be a high-tech environment where it would minimise contact and touch. For this, the team ensured the isolation centres had cameras for continuous monitoring without increasing people in the centres. Even the healthcare staff had to be protected because of the nature of the infection. There was a sudden need of this activity across its hospital chain.

M-commerce helped in terms of patient experience, by digitally-enabling patients, family, care providers, and administrative staff. But while the patient is one important part of the healthcare equation, all the others had to be in sync and enabled in terms of experience, quality, and patient-

care standards. This is where Apollo continues to develop predictive and prescriptive algorithms, check lists, machine learning, and balance score cards even in its apathic can lead to improved speed to diagnosis and care pathway. Time to clinical engagement can drastically reduce, and care outcomes can be measured.

M-commerce is predicted and seen as having the potential to change consumer shopping habits. Consumers are now more dependent on digital devices than ever, and mobile devices have become the most preferred channel for the consumers for online shopping. Social media sites like Twitter, Facebook and Pinterest have all introduced "buy buttons" that allow the shoppers to make purchases without having to leave the platform. Many retailers have introduced one-click checkouts on their sites. The shoppers can enter the payment information once, and then they can use the one-click option to make purchases without having to re-enter the details.

Mobile commerce, also known as m-commerce, involves use of wireless handheld devices like cell phones and tablets to conduct commercial transactions online. M-commerce involves the commercial transactions that take place via apps or mobile sites. M-commerce can be considered as a subcategory of e-commerce. It is a model where firms or individuals conduct business over the Internet. Many products and services can be transacted via m-commerce, including banking, trading, and purchases of movie tickets, plane tickets, and digital music. The rapid growth of mobile commerce is driven by multiple factors, including increased computing power of wireless handheld devices, more memory capacity, and growth of m-commerce applications. M-commerce enables the users to access online shopping platforms, browse and make purchases conveniently and seamlessly using a mobile device.

Comparison: E-Commerce vs M-Commerce

E-Commerce refers to buying and selling goods and services over the Internet. E-commerce includes all commercial transactions that take place digitally using desktop computers. Here the user has to find a location with an Internet connection. M-commerce specifically refers to transactions done via a smartphone or mobile device. It is strictly using mobile devices like mobile phones or tablets. M-commerce users can transact anywhere provided that there's a wireless Internet provider available in that area. For e.g., if we browse a website selling shoes on a desktop and make a purchase it is an e-commerce transaction. If we access the shoe brand or retailer using an app or mobile site then it is an m-commerce transaction

Benefits of M commerce

Better customer experience: Nowadays customers demand a lot from the companies so it is essential to provide a seamless communication for better customer experience. Customers look for a hassle-free buying using mobile devices to be able to buy whenever wherever they want. A good purchase experience using mobile devices right can open up new channels for business. Mobile applications are optimised to provide a fast and streamlined shopping experience which is easy to navigate and needs only a few clicks. This makes sales and leads easier to achieve as the consumer has a much more enjoyable experience compared to other methods. The main benefit of commerce is that it's quicker, easier and more convenient than other shopping channels.

Improved product discovery: Social media platforms such as meta, instagram and pinterest have all introduced "buy now buttons" which allow shoppers to make purchases without leaving the platform. Customers spend a lot of time on social media sites so m-commerce provides a provision to look into products of their interest at some time.

Better Reach: Mobile commerce helps to enter new markets which could not be explored before. Every customer has a preferred way to shop, be it on their desktop, mobile or through social media, so this is perfect for acquiring new customers in m-commerce sector. New customers can be acquired and can enhance relationship with existing customers.

Ease of access: Customers can use mobile applications to access their preferred stores. They do not have to travel to a physical store. The access to mobile apps and websites is quicker. The customers time and effort are saved. M-commerce platforms offer a new marketing channel that should be taken advantage of. For instance, with a mobile application you have a direct connection to end users, giving an invaluable marketing channel where you can sell products directly to the consumer via their mobile device.

Marketing: M-commerce platforms offer a new marketing channel to promote products and services. For example, with a mobile application the retailers can have a direct connection to end users, so it provides a marketing channel where the products can be directly sold to the consumer via their mobile device. There can be push notifications with the latest deals containing information of the latest products and prices, all this is will allow better targeting customers.

Faster Transaction: Most of the mobile applications are faster than a traditional website so m-commerce offers faster transactions for the customers. Quicker browsing facilities and a better user experience has resulted in increase of sales through mobile devices.

Helps in Boosting Traditional Sales: M-commerce not only benefit online sales but also in-store sales. The consumers using their mobile devices check products and browse what's in store, check for product reviews, pricing options, so with m-commerce platform, businesses can expect to increase sales both in-store and online.

Lower cost and Improve Productivity: Connecting to customers using a mobile app will save money on marketing campaigns. If companies integrate the app with social media, it can reduce social media marketing costs. The cost of developing and maintaining an application is much lower compared to other ecommerce platforms. This saves resources as well as the cost.

Attract new customers: People using their mobile phones most of the time search online for products or services. When there is a mobile optimised site there are chances of attracting new customers. Mobile retargeting allows retailers to target advertisement at customers who visit the website.

More insightful data analytics: M-commerce platforms provide businesses with insightful analytics and allow them to better target their customers and increase sales. Demographic data such as name, salary, location, purchase history can be easily gathered by applying analytics integrated into the mobile software. There are different analytics tools available through m-commerce platforms that give businesses data to understand and target their users.

1.17. ICICI BANK LAUNCH M-PAYMENTS USING M-VISA

ICICI Bank Limited, is one of India's largest private sector banks, it launched a service, that helped customers to use their smart phones and make electronic payments at various physical stores, utility billing, taxi aggregators and many others. This service is based on 'mVisa', a new mobile payment solution from Visa. ICICI Bank is the first bank globally to launch a mobile app based 'mVisa' solution for consumers and merchants. With this service, customers can make cashless payments from their smartphones using their debit card by just scanning a 'mVisa' Quick Response (QR) code at a seller's location without swiping the card at an EDC machine. The customers can complete a transaction at a faster pace and as the card is with the customer it provides for enhanced security.

A customer is simply required to click on the 'mVisa' icon on the home screen of the 'Pockets' app to use this service. The app activates the camera in the phone, automatically allowing customers to scan the QR code and enter their debit card PIN. They had partnered with Visa for this service. So, this introduced a payment solution that will allow cashless payments using smartphones at many more locations than are currently available. There are 570 million debit cards in the country, but only 1.1 million point-of-sale (POS) machines available for card payments. This restricts cashless payments to be made only at a certain category of merchants. Simplification of technology would address this market gap and provide digital payments for multiple services with convenience.

The availability of electronic payments using debit card through mobile phone is a new feature to 'PocketsbyICICIBank', the country's first digital bank. It provided a digital wallet from a bank that allows anyone to download and start transacting instantly. The wallet allowed users to send money using e-mail id, mobile number, WhatsApp or bank account. Users can pay bills, recharge mobiles, book tickets for a show, bus or, send physical & e-gifts, 'Pockets' uses a virtual Visa card which enables the users to transact on any website or mobile application in India. Customers can also request for a physical card to use it at any retail outlet. 'Pockets' has over two million downloads in just a few months since its launch.

M-Commerce categories

There are three main categories of m-commerce:

1. Mobile shopping: Online purchases through online stores.
2. Mobile payments: These are the platforms and services that enable you to send and receive money and process sales transactions.
3. Mobile banking: Banking operations can be enabled using mobile devices through standalone apps on top of their existing websites

The major growth areas in M-commerce are:

- In-app purchasing (such as buying clothes via a retail app)
- Mobile banking
- Virtual marketplace apps(amazon)
- Digital wallets (e.g., Amazon pay, PayPal)
- Mobile ticketing

Areas of usage of m-commerce:

Browsing and buying: M-commerce platforms involve the user to browse apps, click around mobile websites, and make purchases. This occurs via dedicated apps, but can also be done using social media platforms including meta, instagram and snapchat offering purchasing options in-app.

Purchases: M-commerce provides for purchases including ordering food or grocery deliveries, and booking taxis or book movie tickets.

Wallet and app payments: Instead of inputting credit card or debit card details in every individual app, a user's digital wallet can be loaded and the purchase can be made with a single click

Digital content purchase: Subscription based apps are popular on mobile, most common ones are with music and video (Netflix and Spotify). Users pay a subscription fee and get an access to entire library of content from their mobile app.

Disadvantages of m-commerce

1. Issues in rural areas: In rural areas still there is less usage of mobile phones and difficulties are faced to get Internet connection. Many people there are still unaware of facilities of m-commerce.
2. Security concerns and risk of frauds: There are still some risks of frauds and security concerns. Many marketers are not ready to handle the security issues. Customers are wary about losing their personal information.
3. Connectivity issue: Internet connectivity is a major issue in m-commerce.
4. People's Habits: There are many who are not ready to change their habits. They feel they are in their comfort zone and don't want to adapt to the new technology.

Common applications of m-commerce

- M-commerce and mobile marketing: Many organizations advertise their products and offers by sending SMS to consumers. They give reward points to customers to increase their sales.
- Finance: With use of mobile phones people can easily do transactions from anywhere. They can do any payments or receive receipts of any payments done through their mobile.
- Retail: Customers can get details of the product and its prices online. They can make purchases or even get some services online.
- Travel Bookings: Airline, railway tickets and hotel rooms can be booked online through smartphones, this works out very convenient to the user.
- Healthcare: Medicines can be ordered online using mobile phones. Patients can contact their doctors and share their health status. They can get even any medical help needed, making it easier for senior citizens.

- For intraoffice communication: Salespeople often need to check the latest prices and offers on the company's products while they may not be in office. They can access all the information easily through their smartphones.
- For gaming: Online games have gained a lot of popularity. Using smartphones, we can easily access multiplayer games.
- Information: People can get news, stocks updates, cricket scores etc. University exam results dates can be viewed.
- Entertainment: Users can access thousands of TV shows, web series, and movies, all through their portable mobile devices.

H. LOCATION ANALYTICS

Location analytics is also referred to as geoanalytics it applies location data to get more invaluable insights. Retailers, shopping malls, and the education industry include geographic components to the data collected. Location analytics unlock new business insights. This gives a better understanding of business partners, new trends and relationship between data. Adding location to an organisation's analytics allows for greater context in decision-making and provides greater insights that is not usually uncovered using traditional business data.

Need for location analytics

Companies use location analytics to connect physical and digital world and provide safety in their work environment. In the physical spaces technology helps organisations to optimise user experience, sustainability, safety and business success. After the pandemic organisations are stressing on high importance on maintaining a safe environment for people in offices and public spaces. Real time data which can track where people and devices are located and how they behave can help organisations to provide them with better experiences. The usage of technologies like AI, wireless connectivity, sensors, IoT, image analysis and other methods help in understanding customer behaviour, track critical assets, and provide for environmental control. Businesses are highly competitive these days so location analytics will help organisations to give them an edge and look into untapped areas for business success.

Features of location analytics

- Interoperability: Location analytics uses IoT to connect systems and provides for increased access to data. Location analytics benefits can be full-fledged tapped by using a software that brings all location analytics functions from many vendors into a single interface.
- Data Collection: Data is collected from various places including LANs, RFID tags, sensors, network devices. Data collection is useful while tracking location of devices during inventory like in a retail store where products are distributed in various floors.
- Analysis: Once data is collected algorithms are applied to recognise the business outcome desired. For e.g., in a store the customers visiting a particular place is observed and products are re arranged to enhance the sales.
- Customisation: Using location analytics unique content can be created for customers based on the insights gathered about them from the data.

Benefits of Location analytics

Hyperlocal intelligence: Hyperlocal intelligence is the term used to describe the application of big data and analytics to local context. Businesses are using this form of analytics to understand their customers and their surroundings better. They can take better decisions by understanding where the customers are. An example would be a store using location analytics to understand which products are being bought frequently. This information can help to improve marketing, and customer service. Location based insights can use visualisations like heat maps and interact with analysts, users, scientists and developers. This provides for better information management which in turn enhances collaboration among team members and helps to take informed decisions.

Better Customer experience: Location data helps to understand how the customers are navigating in the store. A digital map of the store is created. Customers' movements through the store layout are tracked. A check is done if the store's layout is as per the customer's flow. There are customers who get confused at some points, and finally decide not to shop from this store. Customers get frustrated even the way a merchandise is placed. Location analytics to determine where merchandise should be placed. It not only helps in determining where the items are placed, it is also important to consider how customers shop for such items. When location data is used it provides for a better shopping experience for the customers.

Location intelligence: Location intelligence provides retailers with an opportunity to link their customer's online experience with brick-and-mortar stores. It can align the customers' website visits and browsing history to a person's physical presence in the store, retailers can understand the buyer's behaviour and address their needs in a better manner. Location intelligence provides a link between various fragmented entities such as email address, phone numbers, email, physical addresses and the transactional data and the various digital marketing initiatives associated with that customer. Location intelligence helps in performance intelligence. Retailers can use location intelligence to set better performance benchmarks for individual locations. They can compare the performance from previous years performance or can set a target goal and compare. With location intelligence, store objectives can be defined based on an intelligent analysis of actual profit potential.

Selection of retail site: Retailers can work with dynamic map visualisations to reveal about the populations and demographic groupings using advanced location intelligence. For example, a high-end shoe retailer can explore potential new locations in the context of surrounding areas and traffic patterns. Retailers can quickly fix in, on high-quality sites by visualising the potential location. By studying the competitor's locations, the retailer can get an idea of potential profitability of the proposed site.

Location Analytics: Usage in industries

Location analytics can be used in various industries for business improvements. It can bring improvements in business processes from beginning to end, of manufacturing and services including distribution, logistics and assembly. It can also help improve marketing strategies by using geographical data by targeting the right people with personalised content, understanding their major needs and giving offers in real-time Most of the business processes include location data. All the financial transactions, stock transactions, tracking location, and other transaction location is the most important part of any business's data. More and more organisations are looking for ways to harness their location data. IoT, smart cities, connected vehicles, and smart factories are all latest technology developments that rely on location analytics. Businesses can monitor, analyse, and make decisions at the right time in the context of geography.

Location analytics use cases

Retail industry: The retailers have no reliable data about the customers and market after the pandemic. This is when the location data helps them reopen the store and begin the operations efficiently. It helps them know their customers' better, the inventory to maintain, staff scaling if required during weekends, and how to out beat competition.

Restaurants: The restaurateurs understand about the customers' interests, evolved dining habits, using location data. The marketing activities involve all the activities that engage the customers, and ones which convert them to the potential customers.

Insurance: Companies do a risk evaluation before providing insurance. Here location data helps. A unique identifier is given to a property that is required to insure. It provides for data-driven decision-making. The underwriter extracts the information with the help of the unique identifier and evaluates the risk levels before providing insurance coverage of a particular amount.

Automotive industry: The automotive companies use location data of the customers who visit an automotive retail shop, and express their interest to buy a car may be from a competitor or during an event.

I. SOCIAL MEDIA ANALYTICS

Data scientists, analysts, programmers and all other users know the importance social media. Social media is known by its various channels or websites. The channels can be: Facebook, YouTube, Instagram, Twitter, LinkedIn, and others. Social media analytics is the ability to gather data and find meaningful insights from social media channels that help in taking business decisions. They also measure the performance of various actions that are the result of the decisions taken through social media. Social media analytics makes use of software platforms specially designed that work similar to web search tools. The data about various topics or keywords are retrieved through search queries or use of crawlers that spans across channels. The parts of text which are searched are retrieved, loaded into a database, it is categorised and later analysed to get meaningful insights. Social media analytics monitors social channels, looks for opportunities and identifies the problems. The reporting provides for performance analysis.

Need for Social media analytics

Social media analytics can help organisation in the following ways:

- Identify trends in various brands and offerings in various products
- Understand customer sentiments related to a product, brand or services
- Understand the messages send in social media and the response of customers to the message
- Measure the response of customers to social media promotion of products or services
- Identify the USP of the product or service
- Identify the competitors

- Understand the views of customers and their effectiveness
- Align how the third-party vendors and channels impact the performance

Many business activities are impacted using social media analytics strategies:

- Customer experience: Organisations are shifting from product-led to experience-led businesses. Social media channels can use behavioural analytics to understand the customers future needs and look ways to enhance their loyalty and lifetime value.
- Competitor Analysis: It is essential to understand who the competitors aris always critical. For example, a competitor may be launching a new product that may be a disruptor in the market or some product that has been given a good rating by the customer
- Product development: The customer can be understood better by aggregating the views from tweets, reviews in the websites, Facebook posts. This will help understand what are the problem areas the customers are facing, what new features they look in the existing product or service. This will help improve the existing product or develop a new product
- Branding: social media is used by the majority of people. Natural language processing and sentiment analysis can monitor positive or negative expectations of the customers and this will help to maintain brand health, monitor and provide for market positioning and develop new brand attributes.
- Operational efficiency: Many organisations use social media analytics to improve how to improve monitoring and predicting demand. Vendors, retailers and others use this information to manage inventory and suppliers, reduce costs and optimise resources.

Capabilities of social media analytics

Developing a goal is the first step in effective social media analytics. Goals can range from improve services, increasing profits. After this, topics or keywords can be selected and parameters like a month, year or complete date range can be set. The sources used should also be specified. Sources will be like the responses to YouTube videos, Facebook conversations, Twitter arguments, website reviews. The correct sources are to be chosen. A data set is established based on the goals, topics, parameters and sources. Data is retrieved, analysed and reported through visualisations that make it easier to understand and manipulate.

The analysis can be made more effective using the following capabilities found in social media platform:

Natural language processing and machine learning technologies identify the various entities and relationships existing in unstructured data. Most of the social media content is unstructured virtually. They are useful in deriving meaningful insights.

Segmentation is a commonly used method in social media analytics. It categorises the social media participants based on demographics like age, gender, salary, marital status, and other demographics. It can help identify various influencers in these categories. Messages, initiatives and responses can be put in a better manner and targeted by understanding which categories are interacting on key areas.

Behaviour analysis focuses on different roles like user, prospective user, recommender can be categorised based on customer behaviour. Messages can be targeted based on the roles identified.

Sentiment analysis is used to understand the tone and intention of the customer's comments on social media. NLP (natural language processing) helps to understand the entities and relationships to reveal positive, neutral or negative attributes.

Share of Voice: Even the conversations regarding the products, services, brands and reputation can be classified similarly.

Clustering technique is used to discover hidden conversations and get insights from it. It draws an association between keywords or phrases which appear together frequently and taps new opportunities.

Reporting: Dashboards, visualisation charts, graphs, tables and other tools summarise and share the findings from social media analytics.

Social Media Analytics metrics

1. **Performance metrics:** Measuring the performance of social media marketing efforts is important to understand if the strategic efforts applied are working and where there is a need for improvement. The various performance metrics to track include the following:

   - interactions over a period of time and across platforms and to check if the content posted is engaging the audience;
   - Check if the number of followers is increasing over time and whether it is consistent across all platforms; and
   - CTR (click-through rate) for link clicks on posts to see if it is properly driving traffic from social media channels.

2. **Audience analytics:** The most important aspect of social media strategy is to understand and define the target audience. Understanding the audience will help create a good customer experience using the content being targeted at what the customers want and what they are searching for. Earlier it was very difficult to measure the audience data as it was scattered across multiple social media platforms. But with the various analytics tools available now, analysts can analyse data across platforms to understand audience demographics, interests and behaviour in a better manner. AI-enabled tools can help to even predict customer behaviour. They can even study how an audience›s perception changes over time. The better targeted the content is, the advertising cost will be lesser and the cost-per-click of ads can be optimised.

3. **Competitor analytics:** To understand the performance metrics, it's necessary to understand the competitors and their performance. With social media analytics tools, social media performance can be compared to competitors' performance and this will determine what can be improved. Most of the present analytics tools that include AI capabilities can benchmark competitor performance by industry to determine a good starting point for social media efforts.

4. **Paid social analytics:** If the content and targeting isn't right then it will work out very expensive. Advanced analytics tools can predict which content will be most effective and which will be a less risky investment. A platform like say all in one will be best choice to track performance of all social media accounts like Facebook posts, Linked in Ads, Twitter posts. It can track total clicks, total number of active ads, total ad spends, cost per click, cost per engagement, cost per action, cost per purchase. These metrics will help to know exactly where the funds are going to be spent and how much will be the ROI based on the social media efforts. This can also be compared against competitor spending to know that the spending is at an appropriate level.

5. **Influencer analytics:** Social media influencers are part of campaigns to get a competitive edge. The key metrics needs to be measured to achieve the goals of influencer marketing.

   Social media analytics helps to get insights into the right metrics to ensure that influencer campaigns are successful.

   Some influencer metrics that should be tracked include the following:

   - Total number of interactions per 1,000 followers to understand if they're properly generating engagement;
   - Audience size and most frequently used hashtags
   - Number of posts created by influencers on a regular basis
   - Past collaborations

6. **Sentiment analysis:** Sentiment analysis is used to measure whether a campaign, product or service is gaining favourably with the audience. The engagement rate needs to be tracked to ensure the campaign is aligned with the target audience. If there is a drop in the engagement rate there needs to be a change in the course of action. Analysing customer sentiment will help to understand what content has a positive impact on customers. In case a negative sentiment is found it needs to be rectified as soon as it is detected. Social media analytics tools Examples of social media analytics tools include Sprout Social, Google Analytics, Hootsuite and Buffer Analyse.

J. CONTENT ANALYTICS

Content analytics is applying business intelligence and business analytics to digital content. Content analytics is also known as content intelligence. It is measuring and analysing visitor traffic and their engagement with the content published in the form of blogs, articles, and podcasts. The set of technologies used in content analytics processes the digital content and monitors the the way the consumers behave with the consumption and engagement with different types of content like blogs, documents, social media discussions, news sites, online engagement rates. Content analytics metrics include pageviews, engaged time, social interactions (for example, Facebook shares and Twitter retweets), conversions, acquisition sources, and more.

Content analytics is a category of analytics tools which are specifically built to serve the needs of the content teams. The content created is made valuable to teams involved in SEOs, sales promotions, digital publishing and other areas. It provides a mechanism to accurately measure the web engagement sessions along all channels providing a holistic view. This measurement helps to understand which content works well with the audience and they can use this as a basis for developing further content.

Content analytics as defined by Gartner as "*Content analytics is a family of technologies that processes digital content and user behaviour in consuming and engaging with content, such as documents, news sites, customer conversations (both audio and text), and social network discussions, to answer specific questions.*"

In other words, content analytics as defined by Gartner consists of a set of tools and applications used by businesses to make sense of the large amount of data which is generated in the form of digital content across various platforms, mainly the internet. Social media sites, public websites, and customer communications can provide organisations with detailed and extensive information about the factors that affect their performance and results. Businesses make use of AI tools powered by natural language processing (NLP) capabilities to extract meaningful information for usage of content analytics. The tools help in identifying hidden trends and patterns which can help businesses discover information which they did not have an access to. This helps in identifying and solving all major problems and tap new opportunities.

Importance of Content Analytics

Content analytics helps to understand the value a content delivers to the customers. Helps understand which content works best in acquiring, retaining and engaging customers. It gives clarity and insights on the content.

Content vs Web Analytics

The main difference between content analytics and traditional web analytics is that web analytics provides for accessing insights around content easier and simpler for non-technical users. Web analytics was initially designed for e-commerce and product analytics and Content analytics was built for content teams and content-driven businesses. Web analytics tools can be made to work for content analytics, but the content analytics functionality has to be developed by tan individual or the team itself which every individual or team cannot do. Web analytics tools mainly focus on what happens on the website, whereas content analytics helps the teams (marketers and publishers etc) to get a holistic view of how content performs across various platforms and channels. Content analytics tools are also more user-friendly for content creators and non-analysts.

Benefits of content analytics

Access more actionable metrics and insights

On every content that is published, there is data to understand how the audience is responding. Content analytics gives you access to insights which are more attainable than what traditional web analytics tools offer. Let us take some examples:

- **Content conversions:** Understand which content on the site is leading to the most action from the audience and how some portions of the content are most valuable to the customers

- **Referrals through Search:** Identify content that performs well on search engines and drives organic traffic back to your site.
- **Audience engagement time**: Understand how much time the audience are engaged with your content
- **Segmentation of channels:** Trace how each portion of content performs along multiple platforms

Goal Tracking, Reporting, tagging automated

Traditional web analytics tools need the analysts to do more tasks by setting up content reporting, tagging, and goal tracking for creative content teams. In case of content analytics, they automate the tasks.

Goals Tracking: Provides for ease of reporting and tracking KPIs by providing the teams a way to monitor and track the goals for their content. The team needs to align around shared KPIs so everyone can check the progress.

Content reporting: Automatically generates content specific reports about the top contents, popular contents. This report will be a kind of recurring report. Helps the organisation to answer queries about the site and audience.

Smart Tags: Uses ML and NLP and automates subject-matter content tagging. Smart tags scan pages and posts and determine which are the relevant topics and tags are automatically assigned based on the contents.

Get success in business with content analytics: Content analytics is the best way to evaluate the content strategy and check where changes are required to be made. A check on KPIs can be kept aligning to the content strategy.

Content Analytics Strategy

Metrics commonly used

1. **Consumption Metrics:** Includes visitors, page views, subscriptions, time spend
2. **Retention Metrics:** New visitors, returning visitors, bounce rate, count of followers and subscribers

3. **Lead Metrics:** Talks about the attributes that lead to specific campaigns
4. **Sharing Metrics:** Includes website shares, social shares, and blog shares
5. **Sales Metrics:** Includes reports according to analytical needs to measure sales and revenue generated

Conduct content analytics

The following are the key areas in reporting which is included in content analytics:

1. **Production:** Refers to all the content created for the business. Can consider the content by category, type or persona
2. **Engagement:** Refers to the amount of social activity the content attracts. It tracks comments, total shares, links
3. **Performance:** Refers to the extent a portion of content was effective, profitable and helps to align with the goals Tracks top categories, top posts
4. **Content scoring:** Refers to study effectiveness of a content, how many leads got converted

Content Analytics software

SEMrush, WordPress, Unstack

HelloFresh is a meal kit delivery service that allows customers to choose from a variety of recipes and receive a weekly box filled with all the ingredients and instructions they need to make those recipes for themselves. According to HelloFresh copywriter Jacqueline Parisi, their content team had basically been flying blind before using Parse.ly. "It was cumbersome to dive into the depths of the Google Analytics world to find insights worth sharing or acting upon, so data got deprioritized."

K. SENTIMENT ANALYSIS

Sentiment analysis, uses data mining, ML, AI and linguistics to analyse the text for understanding the sentiments like if it is positive, neutral or negative. It is also referred to as opinion mining. Sentiment analysis is basically an approach to NLP (natural language processing) which recognises the emotional tone incorporated in the body of text. The organisations use this method to find the customers views on the products, brands, services. Using Sentiment analysis organisations can get an insight into the sentiments of the customer in real-time, Text analytics uses online sources such as emails, blogs, online reviews, customer support tickets, news articles, chats, tweets to analyse. Algorithms are used to implement rule-based, automatic or hybrid methods of scoring whether the customer is expressing positive words, negative words or neutral ones. Sentiment analysis in addition to knowing the sentiments can help to understand the amount of positive and negative responses, customer d opinion. It helps to analyse various parts of text, such as a full document or a paragraph, sentence or subsentence. Organisations that use these tools to analyse sentiment can review customer feedback regularly and respond proactively to changes of opinion within the market.

Working – Sentiment analysis

Sentiment analysis generally follows these steps:

1. **Data Gathering:** The text that needs to be analysed is identified and collected. This involves usage of a web scraping tool or bot or a scraping application programming interface.
2. **Data Cleansing:** The data is processed and cleansed to remove portions of text that are irrelevant to the text sentiments. This includes contractions, like I'm, and words which convey little information such as *is*, articles such as *the*, punctuation. This is called data standardisation.
3. **Extraction**: the bag-of-words technique is used that tracks the occurrence of words in a text or the word-embedding technique which uses neural networks to find words with similar meanings.
4. **Use of ML model:** The text uses an automatic, or rule based or hybrid ML model. Rule-based systems perform sentiment analysis based on predefined, lexicon-based rules and are often used in domains such as law and medicine where a high degree of precision and human control is needed. Automatic systems use ML and deep learning techniques to

learn from data sets. A hybrid model combines both approaches and is generally thought to be the most accurate model.

5. **Sentiment classification.** Once a model is chosen and used to analyse a portion of text, it assigns a sentiment score to the text including positive, negative or neutral. Organisations can also decide to view the results of their analysis at different levels, including document level, which is mostly used for professional reviews and coverage; sentence level for comments and customer reviews; and sub-sentence level, which identifies phrases or clauses within sentences.

Sentiment analysis is an important way for organisations to understand how customers perceive and experience their products and brands. Most of the customer feedback is given online through a variety of unconnected platforms, such as product reviews and posts on social media forums. Organizations use this feedback to improve their products, services and customer experience. A proactive approach to incorporating sentiment analysis in product development can lead to improved customer loyalty.

The benefits of sentiment analysis include the following:

Tracking real-time customer feedback and sentiment about an organisation's brand, products and services.

- Providing feedback on ways to improve products, services and customer experience.
- Getting data and feedback on problems with products and services.
- Gathering data and feedback that keeps customer support staff up to date on customer issues and improves their ability to respond.
- Tracking the effectiveness of customer support through support tickets and other online feedback.
- Automating customer service by identifying customers' sentiments and automatically sending them to relevant FAQ responses for resolution.
- Identifying emerging marketing trends, and understanding and improving what marketing strategies resonate with customers.

- Gaining competitive insights by monitoring comments about competitors.
- Establishing consistent criteria for evaluating sentiment instead of relying on subjective human analysis.
- Identifying and reacting to emerging negative sentiments before they escalate.

Challenges with sentiment analysis

Challenges associated with sentiment analysis typically include the following:

1. **Neutral sentiments:** Comments with a neutral sentiment pose a problem for systems and are often misidentified. For example, if a customer received the wrong size shirt and submitted a comment, "The size was medium," this could be identified as neutral when in fact it should be negative as the customer had placed for a small size shirt.
2. **Unclear language:** Sentiment doesn't understand the context or tone. If the Answers to a survey question is like "nothing" or "everything" it is very hard to categorise when the context is not given; they can be labelled as positive or negative depending on the question. This is known as lexical ambiguity.
3. **Unclassifiable language:** Computer programs have difficulty understanding emojis and irrelevant information. In case it has to be used the models must be trained with emojis else they will flag texts improperly.
4. **Ambiguous sentiments:** People can give contradictory comments in their statements. A review may have both positive and negative comments. This situation needs to be managed by analysing sentences one at a time. Sometimes a single sentence can contain two contradictory words, and the analysis tools can get confused. For example, "The packaging was terrible but the product was really good."
5. **Named-entity recognition:** When an algorithm cannot recognize the meaning of a word in its context.

6. **Small data sets:** Sentiment analysis tools work best when analysing large quantities of text data. Smaller data sets often won't provide the insight needed.

7. **Language evolution:** Language is constantly changing, especially on the internet where users are continually creating new abbreviations, acronyms, and using poor grammar and spelling. This level of variation and evolution can be difficult for algorithms.

8. **Fake reviews:** Algorithms can't always tell the difference between real and fake reviews of products, or other pieces of text created by bots.

9. **Need for human intervention:** Gartner finds that even the most advanced AI-driven sentiment analysis and social media monitoring tools need human intervention in order to maintain consistency and accuracy in analysis.

Vendors that offer sentiment analysis platforms include Brandwatch, Critical Mention, Hootsuite, Lexalytics, Meltwater, MonkeyLearn, NetBase Quid, Sprout Social, Talkwalker and Zoho.

L. ETHICAL CONSIDERATIONS IN BUSINESS ANALYTICS

Ethics is a moral principle that somehow guides a person on what is bad and what is good. Azim Premji has turned a family-run FMCG business into an FMCG and IT powerhouse. He also believes in contribution to the welfare of society and is involved with Azim Premji Foundation and University. He has built a reputation for himself as well as his organisation as an employer and corporate citizen par excellence. His success is due to his own approach to ethics and also the reason why Wipro is considered to be among the most ethical corporations not just in India but globally. According to Azim, "The real threat to business is from within, from poor ethical standards and lack of integrity that can do incalculable harm. History has proven repeatedly that business ethics, shared value, and corporate governance determine the longevity of an enterprise. What is required is 'capacity building' towards deeper ethical behaviour. Employees must know compliance is not a tick-box activity and they ought to witness their organisations transcend compliance and infuse ethical practices into everyday action. They need to be empowered to thwart unethical action at work and appreciate the fact that business integrity is directly related to the future of the company, their families, and that it securitises their livelihoods."

We need to think now is it right for organisations to gather customer and other data. The answer is no they cannot without consent. Organizations claim to gather data to understand their customers and do target marketing which helps them in personalisation. This personalization according to them provides customer benefits like when we visit a website multiple recommendations pop up. But the question is is it right to capture data without the customer being aware and other than target marketing what else could their data reveal about them? And to what extent is that data being used? Who decides the demarcation is it the customer or the organisation?

Major Issues

- Privacy which can be protected by limiting the data gathered. Make changes in the data in such a way that it is less revealing and there is restricted access to data to ensure privacy of data.
- Informed consent whereby users are fully aware of the purpose of the gathering the data and how it will be used in present and in future. This may save embarrassment for organizations as well as customers who for instance, unknowingly fill out customer data only to find themselves being targeted for some marketing campaigns of which they did not want to be
- An absence of any anonymous terms that will help masking or removal of any portions that might identify a person.

Ethical Framework

Organisations can follow some framework to solve these problems. The features considered include:

- Beneficial – Does use of data benefit consumers as much as it benefits the company?

- Progressive – Does the organisation have a culture of continuous improvement and data minimization?
- Sustainable – Are the insights identified with data sustainable over time?
- Respectful – Have the organisation been transparent and inclusive?
- Fair – Have the company thought about the potential impacts of data usage on all interested parties?

CONCLUSION

As analytics has evolved over a period of time with various applications which are beneficial, it is also important to focus on the way the data is being used and follow the ethical and legal aspects. Applications are built from the data provided by business, social media, m-commerce among others.

POINTS TO BE REMEMBERED

Analytics applications would evolve as per the need and availability of data in organisations. The management is expected to be dynamic in their thinking process so that they are not left behind in the current digital era.

KEYWORDS

Intelligent Agents
Machine Intelligence
Text Mining
Web Analytics
Location Analytics
Content Analytics
Sentiment Analysis
Social Media Analytics

MULTIPLE CHOICE QUESTIONS

1. In supply chain management AI can be used to help businesses

   a. Reduce the number of logistic managers
   b. Make expensive products
   c. Optimise route planning and inventory management
   d. Remove inventory control mechanisms

2. The major benefit of AI in customer service is

   a. Enhance cost of operations
   b. Reduce number of customers
   c. Understand customer preferences
   d. Track customer data without consent

3. AI is used in finance industry for

   a. Social media content creation
   b. Inventory management
   c. Campaign optimisation
   d. Algorithmic trading

4. Which of the following is a commonly used AI application in human resources in the area of recruitment?

   a. Predictive maintenance
   b. AI powered resume screening
   c. Real time inventory monitoring
   d. Sales monitoring tools

5. In competitive intelligence, which ML technique is used for segmenting competitors based on marketing strategies

   a. Market Basket analysis
   b. Decision Trees
   c. K-means clustering
   d. Regression

6. The following is the use of ML in competitive intelligence

    a. Identify the competitors
    b. Get information about competitors from their sites
    c. Create competitors profile
    d. All the above

7. AI powered tools track competitors pricing strategy by the following

    a. Check customer preferences on pricing
    b. Scraping competitors' websites and analysing prices over time
    c. Adjustment made to pricing models
    d. Send updates about prices to all customers

8. The following makes use of NLP to extract useful information and gain insights from unstructured data

    a. Web Mining
    b. Content Mining
    c. Spatial Mining
    d. Text Mining

9. A text mining technique which determines the positive, negative and neutral sentiment expressed in text is

    a. Association
    b. Clustering
    c. Sentiment Analysis
    d. Data Modelling

10. NLP technique used to break down text into smaller units is

    a. Naming
    b. Lemmatisation
    c. Tokenisation
    d. NER

11. Analysing the structure of sentences and phrases to determine the role of different words is

    a. Parsing syntax
    b. Tokenisation
    c. Tagging
    d. Named Entity recognition

12. In Web analytics what is tracked to measure Website traffic?

    a. Website design
    b. Number of email subscribers
    c. Number of visitors and how many returning visitors
    d. Number of email subscribers

13. The Web analytics metric which measures percentage of visitors who leave the page after viewing only a page is

    a. Conversion rate
    b. Bounce Rate
    c. Exit Rate
    d. Entry Rate

14. In location analytics proximity analysis is

    a. Find relation between geographically close locations
    b. Tracking customers in various area
    c. Evaluate trends over a period of time
    d. Study interaction between customer and the sites

15. In location analytics what type of data is commonly used?

    a. Text data
    b. Financial data
    c. Spatial Data
    d. Social media data

Answers

1. c. 2. c. 3. d. 4. b. 5. c. 6. d. 7. b. 8. d. 9. c. 10. c. 11. a. 12. c. 13. b. 14. a. 15. c

CONTENT QUESTIONS FOR DISCUSSION

1. What is the primary goal of text mining?
2. What technique is commonly used to reduce words to their root forms in text mining?
3. What is the bag-of-words model used for?
4. What is web analytics primarily used for?
5. Name one key metric tracked in web analytics.
6. Which machine learning technique is frequently used for sentiment analysis?
7. How does m-commerce differ from e-commerce?
8. Why is ethics important in analytics?
9. What are the various applications of AI in businesses?
10. What are the various types of intelligent agents?

EPILOGUE

The chapter discussed the various trends of analytics in businesses. Applications are varied and wide spread and organisations can explore the potential based on their data availability and skill sets which is needed to conduct the analysis.

CONNECT TO THE NEXT

The book concludes here after addressing various concepts on analytics – from types of analytics, data summarization, data visualization, types of data sources, machine learning techniques, trends in analytics and the important ethical considerations.

REFERENCES

https://www.businessworldit.com/ai/artificial-intelligence-in-business/
https://www.deeplearning.ai/resources/natural-language-processing/
https://www.optimizely.com/optimization-glossary/web-analytics/
https://codersera.com/blog/what-is-m-commerce-and-its-types/
https://www.tibco.com/reference-center/what-is-location-analytics

https://www.unstack.com/blog/content-analytics

https://www.lg.com/global/mobility/press-release/lg-embraces-digital-transformation-with-ai-validation-platform-for-automotive-parts.

https://news.sap.com/2023/05/sap-sapphire-business-ai/

https://yourstory.com/2018/01/business-leaders-on-ethics

https://www.icicibank.com/about-us/article/news-icici-bank-launches-instore-mobilebased-payments-with-mvisa-20150810143242294

https://www.techcircle.in

https://www.netsuite.com/portal/resource/articles/data-warehouse/text-mining.shtml